Be More Assertive

In memory of my dear friend Fay Hutchinson, the very model of an assertive person – delightful, charming, firm but fair. And with thanks to three women who were so very helpful while I wrote this: Linda Blair, who reminded me how to walk the talk; Emma Marlin, whose kind and thoughtful intervention opened a door for me; and Victoria Roddam, the editor we all hope to have!

Teach®
Yourself

Be More Assertive
Suzie Hayman

For UK order enquiries: please contact Bookpoint Ltd,
130 Milton Park, Abingdon, Oxon OX14 4SB.
Telephone: +44 (0) 1235 827720. Fax: +44 (0) 1235 400454.
Lines are open 09.00–17.00, Monday to Saturday, with a 24-hour
message answering service. Details about our titles and how to
order are available at www.teachyourself.com

For USA order enquiries: please contact McGraw-Hill Customer
Services, PO Box 545, Blacklick, OH 43004-0545, USA.
Telephone: 1-800-722-4726. Fax: 1-614-755-5645.

For Canada order enquiries: please contact McGraw-Hill
Ryerson Ltd, 300 Water St, Whitby, Ontario L1N 9B6, Canada.
Telephone: 905 430 5000. Fax: 905 430 5020.

Long renowned as the authoritative source for self-guided
learning – with more than 50 million copies sold worldwide –
the **Teach Yourself** series includes over 500 titles in the fields of
languages, crafts, hobbies, business, computing and education.

British Library Cataloguing in Publication Data: a catalogue record
for this title is available from the British Library.

Library of Congress Catalog Card Number: on file.

First published in UK 2010 by Hodder Education, part of
Hachette UK, 338 Euston Road, London NW1 3BH.

First published in US 2010 by The McGraw-Hill Companies, Inc.

This edition published 2010.

The **Teach Yourself** name is a registered trade mark of
Hodder Headline.

Typeset by MPS Limited, a Macmillan Company.

Printed in Great Britain for Hodder Education, an Hachette UK
Company, 338 Euston Road, London NW1 3BH, by CPI Cox &
Wyman, Reading, Berkshire RG1 8EX.

The publisher has used its best endeavours to ensure that the URLs
for external websites referred to in this book are correct and active
at the time of going to press. However, the publisher and the author
have no responsibility for the websites and can make no guarantee
that a site will remain live or that the content will remain relevant,
decent or appropriate.

Hachette UK's policy is to use papers that are natural, renewable
and recyclable products and made from wood grown in sustainable
forests. The logging and manufacturing processes are expected to
conform to the environmental regulations of the country of origin.

Impression number	10 9 8 7 6 5 4 3 2
Year	2014 2013 2012 2011

Acknowledgements

Thanks to Marianne Williamson for permission to use an excerpt from *A Return to Love* © Marianne Williamson 1992 and to Peter Dale Wimbrow Jr for permission to use 'The Guy in the Glass' © Dale Wimbrow 1934.

Contents

Meet the author

Few of the people who know me were surprised when I said I was writing a book on assertiveness. 'Oh well – right up your street!' was the general response. I come across as a pretty assertive person. And most of my work takes place in areas where you'd assume assertiveness isn't just preferable but absolutely obligatory.

I trained as a teacher, worked for the Family Planning Association and Brook Advisory Centres as press and information officer and then moved into being a freelance journalist. I became agony aunt of *Essentials* magazine, then *Woman's Own* and BBC Health Online and have written columns for the Saturday *Guardian* and *The Times*. I now write a family advice column in *Woman* magazine. I trained with Relate to become a counsellor, and Triple P (Positive Parenting Programme) to become an accredited parenting educator and I am a spokesperson and trustee for Family Lives, the major UK parenting charity, and a trustee of The Who Cares Trust, for 'looked-after' children. I'm one of the founding agony aunts in the Kids In The Middle alliance, lobbying for increased support for children caught up in family breakdown, and edit the KITM website. I make frequent appearances on national and local television and radio, as a counsellor and agony aunt, on programmes such as *BBC Breakfast*, *Woman's Hour* and *You and Yours*, and am a regular on BBC 5 Live, BBC Scotland and BBC Wales. I'm also an occasional presenter on my local BBC radio station, BBC Radio Cumbria. I presented my own series on BBC1, *Stepfamilies*. This will be my twenty-eighth published book and I write features, mainly on relationships, parenting, counselling, health and sex matters, for a wide range of national magazines and newspapers – most recently *The Times*, *The Independent* and the *Guardian*. I have conceived and written leaflets and website material for Parentline Plus,

the NSPCC, One Parent Families, the Family Planning
Association, Parenting UK and Brook Advisory Centres and
contribute an agony page voluntarily to 'Who Cares?', the
magazine for kids in care produced by The Who Cares Trust.
I am regularly asked to give expert comment in national and
local media, and to speak at conferences and give seminars on
a wide range of issues to do with relationships and parenting.

Not exactly the profile of a shrinking violet, is it? But the first time
I stood up in public to speak I made an absolute mess of it. On
my initial forays into media appearances I'd turn up with sheaves
of notes, a dry mouth and shaking knees. And when I talked with
other people, rather than leading I dominated; sometimes, the
last view heard was mine simply because other people were too
blown away to come back with their twopenny worth. I've never
been one to hold back, but it wasn't always effective or sensitive
to other people's feelings, because I wasn't assertive. One of
the lessons assertiveness taught me was to let other people have
their say and to refrain from leaping in like a thundering rhino.
It taught me the value of self-esteem and self-confidence and
the trick of knowing when to come forward and when to wait.
Learning how to be assertive helped me see:

- *It's a skill you learn, not a talent you're born with.*
- *Everybody could benefit from gaining assertiveness skills,
  not just those who feel they don't get a fair hearing
  from others.*
- *It's as much about what you feel inside as what you
  show outside.*

I would say, now, that yes, I'm an assertive person. So, yes,
writing this book to help you gain those skills is right up my
street. But it is so, most of all, because I know it's a process
and a slow one and because I've done the work myself. Before
I could talk the talk, I had to walk it. Learning how to be
assertive doesn't happen overnight and it can be tough as you go
along. I can remember my partner grumbling about some of the
things I was beginning to do differently, and my stepson once

burst out 'Don't you try all those bloody techniques on me! I know what you're doing – it's that damn course, isn't it?' But I stuck with it and both came round. I can honestly tell you if you make that journey it will transform your life – your working life, your family life, your personal life – as it did mine, and for the better.

Suzie Hayman

Only got a minute?

To be assertive is to be confident, positive and self-assured. It means being able to say what you feel and think in an open, honest and direct way. Being assertive allows us to take responsibility for ourselves and our actions without judging or blaming other people, and without making them feel bad. What it is *not* is aggression or manipulation. Being assertive doesn't mean behaving like some of the people who might have led you to think 'I really need to stand up for myself more!'

Assertiveness isn't only pleasanter than fighting and much nicer than always giving in, it's a more efficient way of behaving, too. What you need is to accept and recognize and acknowledge that you matter. You have as much right as anyone else to have what you need and want. Not more and certainly not less – but as much.

Being assertive is not a natural response. We have evolved when under threat to respond with 'fight or flight'. Being assertive means learning to overcome this instinctive and often inappropriate reaction. To be assertive, you need to retrain yourself and to learn a toolbox of strategies, ideas and approaches to help yourself.

Probably the most important strategy you need to learn to become assertive is to use 'I'. We make 'You' statements for several reasons. 'Look what you made me do' or 'You make me so angry!' blames the other person for what has happened and lets us off the hook. A statement such as 'Everyone thinks you're lazy' avoids taking responsibility for angry or critical remarks by saying they belong to someone else. When being assertive, you need to own what you say. Being assertive is standing up for what you feel, think and mean in a direct statement of your feelings and needs.

A useful formula to use is to say:

When... (Describe the situation or behaviour that is troubling you.)

I feel... (Say how it makes you feel.)

Because... (Say what it is about the situation or behaviour that upsets you.)

What I would like is... (Explain what you would like to be different.)

Introduction

- ▶ *Do you feel you've lost, or never had, control?*
- ▶ *Do you feel no one ever listens to you?*
- ▶ *Do you feel your opinion, thoughts, feelings, needs don't matter?*
- ▶ *Do you think everyone else is more important or has more say or more rights than you?*

Unless you've answered a resounding 'no', 'never', 'absolutely not' to every one of those questions, this book is for you! All of us, at some time or other, need a boost to our self-confidence. We've often been taught that to be acceptable we have to be polite, nice and give way. The only problem with that is it tends to lead to your being a doormat. If you've said 'yes' or even 'maybe' to any of the above, what you may need is to become more assertive.

What is assertiveness? To be assertive is to be confident, positive and self-assured. It means being able to say what you feel and think in an open, honest and direct way. Being assertive allows us to take responsibility for ourselves and our actions without judging or blaming other people, and without making them feel bad. When you are assertive you know that you are as important as anyone else – not more, not less but equally – and that you have rights as well as responsibilities.

What it is *not* is aggression or manipulation. Being assertive means standing up for yourself, but not to the disadvantage of other people. It means helping each of you to come away from an encounter feeling that you have been heard and understood. It's not about winning or losing arguments or about getting your own way. It is about making choices and feeling good about them. *Be More Assertive* will help you, whether at home with partner or family, out and about with friends or members of the public or at work with colleagues, to find a better way than the usual one of winners and losers. Instead of confrontation, assertive people use negotiation to smooth a way through life without either imposing on others or allowing others to impose on them.

Becoming assertive is not about taking over or insisting you must have what you want. It is about resisting being controlled or dictated to, put down or ignored. If your self-confidence is shaky, you'll find assertiveness skills particularly useful to help you reassess your self-image and raise your self-esteem. *Be More Assertive* will emphasize the value of clear, calm, frank communication as a means of establishing relationships in which everyone knows where they stand and no-one feels ill-used. You'll find the help you need to state your case and make your point, whether you want to be positive and agree or need to step back and disagree. Using tips and strategies, explanations and illustrative stories, *Be More Assertive* will help anyone, whether at home or in work, to practise being composed, clear-cut and in control. Practical activities will allow readers to rehearse expressing their views, opinions and ideas and to listen to the views, opinions and ideas of others. Readers will also learn to recognize when and how to use assertiveness strategically, because sometimes it's necessary to step away and *not* be assertive!

How long will it take you to get to the end of the course and be a perfectly assertive person? The simple answer is – maybe never. Self-development and change are journeys that tend to go on – you never arrive. No one is, can or should be 100 per cent assertive all the time. Sometimes you have to accept that assertiveness skills will get you nowhere and it's better to retreat or accept the situation. Sometimes we may trip and behave aggressively. The trick is to make the latter a lapse – we can all slip at times – and the former a choice – sometimes it is appropriate to take a back seat.

Our level of self-confidence tends to show in the way we behave. You might be passive – and that tends to go with low self-confidence. When you behave passively, you allow aggressive people to harm you, push you around, tell you what to do and what to think. Imagine an invisible wall around you – that's your personal boundary. Boundaries are important because they protect you. When you let down your boundary, you let people influence you or affect you. You want to have a boundary that lets in the people you love and trust and keeps out the people you'd prefer to be at arm's length. Passive people find it hard to defend their own personal boundaries and thus allow anyone to tell them what to do and think. If you're passive, you are also not likely to risk trying to influence anyone else. Aggressive people do not respect the personal boundaries of others. They charge on in, rolling over boundaries and not only seizing control but forcing their own feelings and opinions on the people around them. They may not mean to do harm but are careless about it because their main aim is to be Number One and Top Of The Heap, and to have their own way. You may think that aggressive behaviour goes hand in hand with high self-confidence, but that's not always true. It might go with arrogance – an assumption that you know what's best and should be the centre of attention. But actually, all of that is more akin to a lack of self-confidence than an excess of it. If you have to shout or put someone down to make your wishes known, it's because you don't have real self-assurance. Standing on someone's shoulder may lift you above the crowd but it doesn't actually make you any taller.

In contrast, if you have self-confidence you can be assertive. And if you are assertive, you display self-confidence. Best of all, both self-confidence and assertive behaviour can be learned – and that's what *Be More Assertive* offers you. As an assertive person you will speak your mind. You may try to influence others, but you'll do so in a way that offers them the choice and that respects their personal boundaries. You will also be willing and able to hold your own boundary against aggressive moves, standing up for yourself and your rights.

Being assertive is always to your benefit. That doesn't mean, however, that being assertive will result in you always getting what you want. The result of being assertive is that:

- ▶ *you feel good about yourself*
- ▶ *other people know how to deal with you because you are open and authentic.*

Assertive people have the following characteristics:

▶ *They feel free to express their feelings, thoughts and desires.*
▶ *They have control over their emotions.*
▶ *They know their rights.*

They feel free to express their feelings, thoughts and desires
If you are assertive, you feel able to tell other people that something makes you feel upset, happy, confused. You have the self-confidence to go against the crowd in disagreeing with a proposed action or to propose something new. You can tell people what you'd like to happen or what you want to do. In contrast, if you're passive you keep quiet for fear of being shouted down or contradicted and you don't feel able to ask for anything. And if you're aggressive, you blast away, often not telling people what you feel but simply what they are going to do.

They have control over their emotions
We all feel strong emotions. We can be delighted, happy, sexy. We can be angry, envious, jealous. Passive people keep their emotions in check, until they burst out, often self-destructively and at the wrong moment. Aggressive people tend to allow their emotions to run unchecked, as a way of intimidating and controlling others. If you're assertive you recognize and accept negative emotions and deal with them, and you display your positive emotions in a suitable way.

They know their rights
We all have rights and responsibilities. Passive people tend to be heavy on their responsibilities and light on their rights, doing everything for other people and letting their own interests be forgotten. They allow themselves to always be back of the queue. Aggressive people push to the front of the queue, insisting on getting theirs first. They tend not to think of other people and their rights and responsibilities. Assertive people, however, keep the balance. They know what is due them – no more but no less than anyone else. In doing so they take responsibility for themselves rather than always putting other people in front of them, or everyone else always behind them.

Being assertive makes life so much easier. It helps you get on with your partner, your family, the people you work with and those you encounter day to day.

So how can you begin? Here are four tips to start:

1 *Say what you mean.*
2 *Don't take it personally.*
3 *Don't make assumptions.*
4 *Do your best.*

Say what you mean. Starting today, watch the number of times you're vague and evasive and give people the wrong impression because you're scared to say what you really think or feel. Or the number of times you say 'I'm fine', 'Yes, of course I'm happy to do that for you', 'Oh, I agree', when none of it is true. What you're going to be working towards is being kind, caring, tactful... but truthful. 'I'm tired and overworked. I'd really appreciate some help', 'No, I'm sorry, but I can't do that for you' and 'We have different opinions on that' are going to be the things you'll say instead. It may take time, but we'll get there!

Don't take it personally. We often suffer because we assume if people are offhand, angry or controlling it must be because we made them feel so, it was our fault and we should change. When people behave badly it's usually because of something going on with them. What we'll be moving towards is you taking responsibility for your own actions and leaving others to do so for theirs.

Don't make assumptions. Assuming that you can't change, you can't manage this and others won't accept it, gets you stuck. You may be right in thinking it won't happen overnight. Recognizing that you'll have to work at it and that other people may take some time to come round is reasonable. Assuming you're doomed to fail and that it will never be different is not.

Do your best. Nobody can be perfect. You're not trying for perfection but for being 'Good Enough'. This means you can take your time, can make mistakes and that what is right for you and works may vary from time to time and place to place. Avoid judging yourself and your efforts and don't indulge in self-abuse or regrets. Simply, get on with it!

There's a wonderful quote that is often believed to come from Nelson Mandela's inauguration speech. It doesn't – it comes from a book called *A Return to Love* by Marianne Williamson (1992). It speaks to anyone struggling with self-confidence issues, who is about to begin learning how to be assertive:

> *Our deepest fear is not that we are inadequate. Our deepest fear is that we are powerful beyond measure. It is our light, not our darkness, that most frightens us. We ask ourselves, Who am I to be brilliant, gorgeous, talented, fabulous? Actually, who are you not to be? ... Your playing small doesn't serve the world. There's nothing enlightened about shrinking so that other people won't feel insecure around you. We are all meant to shine, as children do ... It's not just in some of us; it's in everyone. And as we let our own light shine, we subconsciously give other people permission to do the same. As we're liberated from our own fear, our presence automatically liberates others.*

You should shine. You should be showing how brilliant, gorgeous, talented and fabulous you really are. *Be More Assertive* is going to help you do just that.

1

Do you want to be assertive?

In this chapter you will learn:
- *the pros and cons of assertive behaviour*
- *what it means to be assertive*
- *why assertiveness could work for you*
- *to understand your and other people's behaviour*
- *to consider with whom you might want to be assertive – family, friends, colleagues*
- *the tools and strategies you might need to become more assertive.*

Do you want to be assertive?

If you feel you've suffered years of being overlooked, pushed around, and having your ideas and needs ignored, 'Do you want to be assertive?' may seem like a silly question. Of course you'd like to be able to speak up and speak out! But if you've been finding it hard to make your voice heard, you do need to consider whether one of the reasons is that you have some reservations about being that assertive person. To choose assertiveness, you first have to consider what you feel is meant by being assertive. You then have to think what you might feel are the drawbacks, as well the advantages, of being assertive.

Being assertive doesn't mean behaving like some of the people who might have led you to think 'I really need to stand up for myself more!' It does not mean always getting your own way; it does not mean always being in charge. Being assertive isn't when your voice is always loudest or your demands always to the fore. Being assertive is not the same as being dominant, hectoring or bullying. You don't have to be that sort of person to be more in control and more forward than you might be now.

THE DOWNSIDES OF BEING ASSERTIVE

But there are some downsides of being an assertive person. These may be what come to mind when you think of making changes and becoming more forward. And these may be what hold you back. If you are assertive, you:

- *must make choices, and acknowledge that not making a choice and doing nothing is a choice in itself*
- *have to take responsibility for yourself and your choices and stand up and say 'Yes, this is what I think and believe, and do'*
- *can't make excuses or hide behind other people – you cannot say 'I couldn't help it' or 'They made me do it' or 'Everyone thinks…' or 'Of course, it's not what I think…'*

THE ADVANTAGES OF BEING ASSERTIVE

If you could be a more assertive person, what advantages might you enjoy? You could:

- *express your opinions, and feel confident in knowing they are as good as anyone else's*
- *express your feelings, and know you have as much right to have them as anyone else*
- *feel in control, and recognize that you have responsibility for your life and your decisions*
- *make choices, and acknowledge that you can do so*
- *get some of what you want, knowing that we can't always have everything we desire or need but have a right to ask anyway*
- *have the right to refuse to do what you don't want.*

What is assertiveness?

We'll look at why other people in your life may resist your becoming assertive, and how to help them see it is to their advantage too. But before we get to that, you need to face up to the resistance you yourself might have. At the same time as wanting to change and knowing you need to change, you could be sabotaging yourself. If I take this step, you may ask yourself, will I become confident? Will I become overconfident? Will I become downright bossy?

Insight

When you make changes to your life, you may come up against opposition. You might expect that from other people but be less prepared for the obstacles you, yourself, may put in your way. It's as important to recognize and be prepared for your own objections as for those of others.

When you talk about wanting to be more assertive, what you might really mean is:

▶ *How can I get people to listen to and take notice of me?*
▶ *How can I stand up to people who push me around?*
▶ *How can I have a little more control over my life in general or some situations in particular?*

To achieve any of these, you don't have to become that bossy person. Bossiness is hardly a helpful behaviour pattern and it's certainly not what I would like to help you practise. But sometimes, words such as bossiness are used by people getting upset that you're no longer a pushover, not because you are doing anything wrong.

Insight

When I was younger, I was often accused of being bossy. It took me many years to untangle what was really going on. Part of the accusation was because I can be overpowering,

(Contd)

and I realized I had become that as a reaction. When you're held down and ignored, sometimes you can come on a bit too strong to be heard at all. But most of it was simply because I was a woman willing to speak up. I wasn't bossy – I was self-confident. You need to watch out for people wishing to cut you down to size, simply because it doesn't suit them for you to be able to hold your own.

But rest assured – becoming assertive doesn't mean you're going to become someone you don't recognize or can't like. You also don't have to blame or beat yourself up for finding it so hard. The fact is that assertiveness isn't necessarily a natural behaviour for us.

Why is it often hard to be assertive?

Being assertive is not a natural response, either in human beings or in other members of the animal kingdom. What all of us have evolved to do in any situation where we feel uncertain or under threat is to go into the 'fight or flight' response. If you think you're in danger, a primitive part of your brain tells you to act, at once. It says you should either step up and attack, or batten down the hatches and get out of there. And to make sure you do so as quickly and efficiently as possible, it floods your body with a cocktail of chemicals that enables you to see clearer, run faster, and fight harder. You feel a rush of adrenaline and your fists may clench, your breathing increases, your face flushes and the hairs on the back of your neck stand on end. You may want to wade in there and have it out. Or you may want to freeze and be as invisible as possible, or to run and hide.

Your primitive brain cannot distinguish between little threats and big ones or even real threats and imaginary ones. It's not subtle but it is quick. The effects of the fight or flight impulse can overwhelm you even before you realize you're feeling stressed. You're flooded with the emotions triggered by that primitive and powerful brain. And this emotional flooding often makes rational thought not just hard but impossible. Instead of thinking things through, and acting in control, you find yourself being pushed to be either aggressive – 'fight', or submissive – 'flight'.

Insight

The instant physical reaction to attack or flee may have worked very well when we were living in caves and any animal or stranger who came in sight was a genuine threat to our survival. It doesn't work when the fight or flight reaction is triggered every time someone steps in front of you in the bus queue or when a friend or colleague or family member annoys you.

OVERCOMING INSTINCT

Being assertive means learning to overcome this instinctive and often inappropriate reaction. Clearly, when you step in front of a bus or when someone does seek to do violence to you or someone you love, you'll be glad of that rush of strength and speed that allows you to react as is needed. But how often does that happen? Not nearly as often as we find the automatic response is triggered. And freezing or running away or hitting out with words or fists is more likely to get us into a miserable situation than save our lives. One reason to become assertive and to learn to overcome the fight or flight response is that assertive behaviour works so much better, whether at home or at work.

Insight

Whether in your job or in your family, what you want to be is someone who gives a good example, who listens and cares and brings out the best in yourself and those around you. Being someone who fights or flees does neither!

Assertive behaviour includes and involves other people, it does not dominate or exclude them. It helps you and those around you grow and develop. Dominating your work colleagues or your family or people you meet in everyday life is not a good management style in any circumstances. It tends to be based on short-term rewards and results – the dominant person has their way and feels they have done the right thing because it seems to work.

DOWNSIDES OF BEING DOMINANT

Being dominant can be beneficial for the person in the lead, but it fails completely to make effective use of the abilities and potential of everyone else. And in fact, it's not much good for the leader either, in the long run. If you only ever get your way because you push, scream and shout yourself into that situation, you may never develop real skills – to assess situations and make the best decision, to lead and inspire others to have their say, to change and to adapt. The day someone else stands up and is a bigger bully than you, you're lost. Use this method in families and you may lose out dramatically. A partner may put up with it for years, and then suddenly opt out. Children may vote with their feet, getting as far away from you as they can as soon as they are able. And even if people stay physically close, you may find they absent themselves emotionally, avoiding intimacy with you.

DOWNSIDES OF BEING PASSIVE

But it's a mistake to think that taking the apparently easy line and not standing up for yourself is any better. Being passive is not a good style to live by, either. Again, it has short-term rewards and results – you may feel it works for you because you keep your head down, stay out of the line of fire, have an easy life with little conflict because you always give in. But constantly buckling under isn't good for you or for the people around you. It means never getting your own needs met and that can lead to buried anger and seething frustration. It means that neither you nor anyone else you encounter has the important chance to learn how to compromise and negotiate – you always step aside for them and let them have what they want.

Using the fight or the flight option is the result of a similar condition – that of having low self-esteem and low self-confidence. You can see how that works with anyone who backs down and seeks to hide or flee, can't you? You may not feel you have the right to make your feelings known, you may feel you don't have the skills to stand up for yourself, you may believe that your views and your needs are not as important as anyone else's.

But in fact, a similar belief also often fuels those who bully their way through life.

> ### Insight
> Those who throw their weight about are usually very insecure people. They dominate because they don't have the confidence to allow other people to have responsibility and influence. And when we back off and allow a person who is bullying to get their own way, the behaviour persists because we're rewarding it.

You may think someone behaves like this because they want to and like it. Often, they simply do it because it works and because once they've started to behave this way, everyone around them reinforces the behaviour by letting them get away with it.

WHY DO WE BEHAVE THIS WAY?

Early childhood experiences play an important part in creating this sort of pattern of behaviour. When children only get attention if and when they scream for it or insist on it they learn that's the way to behave. If they find from experience that when they play quietly or ask nicely they are ignored but when they fight and have tantrums and act up they get noticed, then that's the way they will go on behaving. Bullies are victims as well as aggressors. And although it's a tough challenge for anyone on the receiving end of their behaviour to see them in a positive light, they actually deserve sympathy and help to change to more positive ways of interacting. That's yet another reason for you to become assertive – you'll be helping those people in your life who have such self-destructive behaviour patterns to change to more positive ones.

Don't feel that becoming assertive means totally changing your way of life and your core being. You're seeking to become you – but a you who feels better about yourself and has healthier dealings with those around you. In becoming assertive, you're not going to become a person who throws their weight around, who is always ahead and in charge. And you're certainly not going to become a bully. You'll want to say your piece, to stand by your feelings and beliefs, to defend yourself, to control your own choices and destiny, but not to control others.

Insight

Becoming more assertive is going to help you resist being put down by other people, but not at the price of becoming the person who does the putting down.

IS BEING ASSERTIVE THE SAME AS NAGGING?

As well as being bossy, you may find yourself being accused of nagging as you work towards becoming assertive. Being assertive is not the same as being a nag. But what is nagging? Sometimes, people accuse us of nagging because they don't want it hear what we're saying – please empty the rubbish, clear the table, do your chores, feed the cat, make that call…. It's called nagging when really it's 'Yes I know I should be doing that but I don't want to, so I'll try to make *you* feel bad for asking, to stop *me* feeling bad for not doing it!'

Repeating a request works sometimes. You can repetitively tell a child to do their homework, turn down the music, wash the coffee mug and they may finally go do it. You can ask an adult to make a call, take out the rubbish, pick up their clothes over and over again and they'll probably, at long last, give in. But the chances are next day you'll be back repeating the same old thing because neither of you has learnt anything. What has often happened is that the other person has not, for various reasons, heard our request and we get into a loop of repeating it. While there is one, and only one, circumstance where it can pay off to keep repeating a message (and we'll deal with that later…), on the whole if they aren't listening we need to think it through and change tactics. If you or the person you're addressing feels you're nagging, it's a lost cause. If you find yourself saying any variation on 'But you said…'; 'I told you…'; 'You didn't…'; 'I've asked you a hundred times…'; 'When are you going to…' that's the moment to take a deep breath, regroup and come at it a different way. Part of being assertive is learning when to put your foot down because the other person is using the old 'Stop nagging!' tactic to avoid a reasonable request, and when to jump tracks and use a new strategy.

Case study

Sonia contacted me because she was at the end of her tether. She and her husband ran a busy hotel, they had three children and her elderly mother was becoming an increasing responsibility. When I suggested some work on her ability to be assertive would help, she was horrified. 'I would hate to be one of those people!' she insisted. What sort of people? 'Oh, you know – those bossyboots who tell everyone what to do!' Her father, she explained with great pride, had been someone who knew his own mind and was very successful. Of course, he never had any time for any of his children. Even now, his response to his wife's increasing frailty was to get other people to take care of her. Her mother had been loud and unrelenting – Sonia always felt she had to get it right first time or face a tirade, and she was never good enough. I pointed out that it sounded as if Sonia had two interesting models in what she had assumed was assertive behaviour. In fact, neither was assertive but sounded more akin to aggression or passive-aggression. Sonia didn't want to become like either of them, but when we talked she realized she didn't need to do so. She could become assertive without ending up like either of her parents.

PUTTING THE TOOLBOX TOGETHER

To be assertive, you need to retrain yourself and to learn a toolbox of strategies, ideas and approaches to help yourself. As already said, assertiveness isn't instinctive behaviour. Our instinct is to fight or run. But it is something we can learn to do. Anyone, at any time, in any circumstances can learn assertive behaviour and become comfortable in using it.

▶ *Being assertive is something we learn to do, not are born knowing how to do.*
▶ *Being assertive helps you and it helps the people around you.*

- ▶ *Being assertive makes you feel good about yourself, good about other people and good about what you are asking for.*
- ▶ *Being assertive won't get you everything you want every time but it will get all of you what you need.*

Because it is not instinctive behaviour, it takes some work and some effort to pick up and learn to manage the skills of assertive behaviour. Because it is not instinctive behaviour, you don't need to blame yourself or feel bad about not having those skills at present. Because we are thinking and learning beings, the fact that it is not instinctive behaviour does not mean we are stuck forever with being unassertive. Human beings can learn and change – that's what makes us human. And what we can come to recognize is that a little work and effort now saves time and misery later.

Essential points to consider

1 *Be aware of the changes in your life that becoming assertive can bring.*
2 *Weigh up the pros and cons of these changes before you choose to start.*
3 *Becoming assertive will mean learning to overcome some of your instinctive or inherited responses.*
4 *Look back and realize how early childhood experiences can still have a big effect on how you are now.*

Where and when do you want to be assertive?

Where and when do you want to be assertive? You may have one particular person with whom, or one particular circumstance where, you'd love to be more self-assured. It may be with a spouse or partner, your children, the wider family, friends, work colleagues or clients, neighbours, kids on the street, shop assistants, cold callers, doorsteppers, other customers, people you encounter in all sorts of situations. These may be everyday, regular situations, or unusual and particularly stressful or even dangerous situations. The skills of assertiveness, once learned, can help you in any and all of them.

▶ *Being assertive is the route to self-esteem and respect for ourselves and for others. You feel good about yourself for doing it and good about the people with whom you interact, even if you don't always get exactly what you want.*
▶ *Being assertive is always positive. It is the upside of being strong, protective of yourself and of other people's integrity and rights, of avoiding frustration and irritation, of not getting blocked or stuck, of moving on and finding solutions for problems.*

Why is becoming assertive the right choice?

There are two important and, I think, main reasons why choosing to become assertive is the right thing to do. Some people like to make choices for a positive reason – in other words, there's a reason to go forward into making a change. So here's your positive reason: being assertive feels good.

But you may be someone who prefers to make choices on avoidance grounds – you do things to go backwards away from things you don't like. In that case, one very good reason for avoiding *not* being assertive is that being unassertive feels bad!

There are good reasons also for choosing not to be either aggressive or submissive. Being aggressive gets you what you want at other people's expense. They resent you and do not respect you and look for ways of getting away from or getting back at you. It's hard work and you are on your own. Being submissive is also hard work. We let other people do the work but we feel an emotional toll. Never getting what we want is wearing and dispiriting. We resent instead of respecting or loving the people who dominate us, whether family, friends or work colleagues, and never have truly equal or satisfying adult relationships with them. We never bring out the best in them or ourselves.

PULLING STRINGS BEHIND THE SCENES

There is another pattern of behaviour that often comes about when people don't feel they're getting what they want. If you have made it a habit of standing back and letting other people lead, you may suddenly burst out in aggression, out of frustration and anger. But you may also cultivate another method of getting your own way while still hiding in the shadows and seeming to give in. This is called passive-aggression. Passive-aggression is when we influence and stage-manage people to give us what we want. Classic passive-aggression is the person who says 'Don't mind me – I'll be alright. Yes, you go along and enjoy yourself while I do the clearing up...' It's control by guilt and complaint, and it can work very well. Who doesn't know someone held in thrall by a parent, partner, child, friend or colleague, who plays this game? But being passive-aggressive is equally as unsatisfying as being either submissive or aggressive. We may get what we want but it's by underhand means so we can never really admire or like the people we manipulate or ourselves, nor they us. There may be some satisfaction and a sort of empowerment in pulling people's strings but it is unpleasant and we usually don't feel good about ourselves.

> ### Insight
> Passive-aggression can be a bit like 'crying wolf'. Those who use it often get their way by appealing to your sympathy or your anxiety – do this for me because I'm not well, I can't manage, I need your help. One day, you may get so fed up you refuse to play the game any more and break off contact. Then, when they *really* aren't well, can't manage and need your help, you may refuse, thinking it's just the same old act.

Ten tips to becoming assertive

Assertiveness will improve your life – it's a far better way of behaving than being either passive or aggressive or passive-aggressive. So how can you begin to become assertive? Here are ten tips we'll be working towards. You need to be able to:

1 *Say it like it is.*
2 *Own what you say.*
3 *Walk the talk as well as talk the talk.*
4 *Give praise.*
5 *Accept compliments.*
6 *Don't make it personal.*
7 *Say what you want rather than what you don't want.*
8 *Choose the right time.*
9 *Choose the right place.*
10 *Reward yourself.*

Say it like it is. To make your feelings and wishes known, you're going to learn to be direct and specific. Instead of saying, 'Why do I always have to do everything...', 'You always...', or 'Nobody ever listens to me!', you'll learn to say, 'You left the kitchen in a mess this morning so I'd like you to clear it up now', 'You didn't feed the cat this evening, so I want you to do it now', and 'When I asked you to finish that report you didn't, so I want you to do it now'. Being direct and specific means the other person knows what you're objecting to, why you're upset and what you want done instead.

Own what you say. When we're being unassertive we often try to palm off our feelings and needs on to someone else. We say 'Everyone is upset with you', or 'We would like...', or 'You don't want to be doing that...'. When you own what you say, you use 'I'. We'll learn how to say 'I'm upset and want to talk about this', 'I would like you to...', and 'I would prefer you to do this...'. Once you own what you say, you get far more of what you need and want.

Walk the talk as well as talk the talk. Your words only convey a fraction of your meaning – your stance says much more. You'll learn to use body language that matches and backs up your words. 'I'm really annoyed with you...' doesn't get the message across if you mumble it with crossed arms while looking down at your feet, or say it with a bright smile.

Give praise. If you want to have influence on other people, for every time you have to pull them up for what they have done wrong, you need to find at least two occasions to thank and praise them. We all want approval and we tend to repeat actions that get us noticed positively. It works far better than trying to get people to do what you want by telling them off when they get it wrong.

Accept compliments. One important aspect of assertiveness is knowing your own worth. And that means when someone compliments you saying 'Thank you' and accepting it, not saying 'Oh, I didn't do anything', or 'What, this old rag! I'm sure my bum looks big in it!'

Don't make it personal. When dealing assertively with other people, it is behaviour you may object to and wish to change, not the person. Don't say 'You lazy git!' Instead say, 'I'm upset you didn't wash up. I'd like you to do so now.'

Say what you want rather than what you don't want. It works better to tell a child 'We're going shopping. I want you to stay by me in the supermarket and it will really help me if you hold the list and tick off all the things as we find them', than to say 'We're going shopping and I don't want a repeat of last week where you ran up and down the aisles!' People tend to pick up on the words you use, and in that case all the child hears is 'run up and down the aisles'.

Choose the right time. Trying to have a discussion about who takes out the rubbish, or why the kids haven't done the chores, or a workmate's failings in the workplace, is doomed to fail if you pick the moment when everyone is tired or really busy. Say 'We need to talk…' and agree a time to do so.

Choose the right place. Tackling a touchy teen in their own bedroom may make them feel invaded, and thus aggressive. Summoning someone to your room may put them on the defensive. Doing it in front of other people can upset everyone – it's humiliating for the person you're addressing and embarrassing for onlookers. Pick a neutral, quiet spot.

Reward yourself. Give yourself a pat on the back each time you use an assertive response. Do it whether the other person responded well or not.

Resisting fight or flight

So, how can we begin? First we need to break ourselves of the impulse to strike out or head out when the going gets even the slightest bit tough. You can't stop yourself reacting instinctively with that surge of adrenaline and the feelings it produces. But unlike our primitive ancestors or animals, what we can do is learn to control the behaviour that might follow.

The following five tips will help you remain calm and grounded, avoiding fight or flight, so you can act in a way that is effective and respectful to yourself and to others.

1 *Think before you react.*
2 *Talk yourself through it.*
3 *Mind what you say.*
4 *Mind how you say it.*
5 *Stand tall.*

THINK BEFORE YOU REACT

Your primitive brain will be spurring you on to take immediate action. If there's a sabre-toothed tiger on your tail, or you've walked in front of a bus, that would be wise. In most situations assertiveness rather than fight or flight is called for, and in this case you need to take more time to assess the situation before you respond. Assertive action often calls for thought and reflection, especially when you are new to acting in this way. Pause, think, count to ten and give your thinking brain the chance to catch up with what is actually happening rather than what your primitive brain feels might be happening. Say 'I need to think this through' to people insisting on your doing what they want. If they continue, it's useful to be able to say 'If you want an immediate answer it's no. If you want me to reconsider that, I need some time.'

TALK YOURSELF THROUGH IT

Have you ever looked in a mirror and made a scared face – and then found yourself reacting to what you see by getting frightened? It works! If you tell or show yourself you are scared, or angry, or upset, your emotions will follow suit. If you think the other person is in the wrong, or is going to abuse you, or that you are going to be on the losing end of the encounter, you're likely to experience exactly what you feared. Not because it was necessarily true, but because you talked yourself into it. You gave away your power and control and you invested the other person with it all. You created an unpleasant, scary persona for them, which may not have been true until you began to act to them as if it was.

So in a touchy situation it's important to affirm calm thoughts that put you in control. Reassure yourself you are safe. Tell yourself you are capable and strong. Remind yourself the other person needs your support and understanding. And use Dos rather than Don'ts. If you say 'Don't be angry' or 'Don't be scared' all you may hear are 'angry' and 'scared'. Instead, concentrate on what you want. 'Be calm', 'Listen', 'Be understanding', 'Be firm'.

MIND WHAT YOU SAY

Watching what you say and how you say it is vital if you want to be assertive and defuse any tension. The words we pick can sometimes have the opposite effect to what we want. Telling someone to calm down, for instance, can make them blow up. That's because it may be heard as patronizing, interfering or judgemental. Saying 'I understand....' can lead to an angry 'No you don't...', which is true – you can't really understand what someone else is feeling. Perhaps least helpful of all is to begin anything you say with the word 'you'. 'You should...', 'You must...', or 'You can't...'. A recipe for disaster would be to say 'Calm down. You're really making a fuss about all this. I understand what you're feeling but you should clear up this mess...' Cue shouts, flouncing off and slammed doors!

Instead of the 'You' and 'But', use 'I' or 'And'. Instead of 'I understand', try 'It sounds as if you're having a bad time. I sympathize.' So, 'I appreciate you're upset. I'd like us to talk about it so I can help. I suggest we both take a little time to think it over. And, I would like the kitchen cleared so I can make supper. I suggest we do it together and when we're ready, we can talk.'

Using 'And' builds co-operation and understanding. Using the word 'I' is honest as it tells the other person what you are feeling and what you want, rather than fudging the responsibility or blaming and labelling them. 'You should do that' invites 'Why the heck should I?', while 'I would like you to do that' may well be met with 'Oh. OK.'

Try this

Say what you would like people to do out loud and directly, without apology. It is ineffective to hint that it would be nice if someone would help you, do their chores, finish the job that was theirs, or that the customer services person should

(Contd)

replace the iron that doesn't work or correct the items left undone by the car service. You will undercut yourself and therefore negate what you are asking if you say 'I'm sorry to ask you but...', 'Don't mind me...' 'Sorry to interrupt...'. Pause, think and come out with what you really want and need to say firmly, directly and clearly.

MIND HOW YOU SAY IT

As well as the words, watch your tone. Studies suggest that your tone of voice conveys a major part of your message – as much as 40 per cent. Shouting, speaking in a shrill, high-pitched voice, or talking too quickly, all send the message that you are under stress and tending towards either being submissive or aggressive. Take a deep breath, slow down and keep your voice low, firm and pleasant.

STAND TALL

Being assertive means watching your body language – how you stand, what you do with your hands, the sort of eye contact you make. Whether you realize it or not, your body sends out the major message of your intentions. If almost 40 per cent of what we are really saying is conveyed in our tone of voice, a whopping 55 per cent is communicated by what the other person can see. Your words may be soft, but if your fists are clenched, your finger points, your eyes stare and you loom over the other person, they know they are under threat from aggression. If you hunch over, avoid eye contact, tuck your hands into your armpits or cross your arms, and legs, you're sending out signals that say 'I give in! Walk all over me!'

So make eye contact, but stand or sit at an angle so as not to seem face to face confrontational. Be at the same level, either standing or sitting or crouching down. And keep your body 'open' by avoiding crossing arms or legs and making your hand gestures inviting and inclusive rather than pointing or making fists.

Why would anyone NOT want to be assertive?

Why might we be unassertive? Often, we do it to be liked, loved, approved of, thinking being a Yes person will achieve this while being a No person will not. It may be out of fear – that our desires are so powerful that once we let them out, they may bring everything around us tumbling down. Or someone else might have given us the impression that when we get what we want, it takes away from them, and that this would be selfish and bad. We often perceive standing up for ourselves as being the same as riding roughshod over other people's needs. So we let ourselves have that done to us, instead. It may be out of guilt. There are plenty of circumstances where we can be fooled into thinking that asking for our needs to be taken seriously somehow sets up an undesirable situation. Something in your past – your childhood, after a separation or a death or illness – can leave you feeling 'When I get my own way, all sorts of terrible things happen'.

Do you find yourself saying any of these, to justify and explain non-assertive behaviour?

- *My partner gets angry with me – it's far easier to give in and avoid an argument.*
- *My family won't help around the house and when they do they do it wrong. It takes less time and effort to do it all myself.*
- *I get lumbered with collecting my friend's children from school. I do it far more often than anyone else but I don't want to cause bad feeling by refusing.*
- *My mother insists we have Sunday lunch with her every week. We'd like to do something else sometimes but there's nothing I can do.*
- *The whole family come to me every Christmas and I'm expected to do it all. I don't have a good reason to refuse but I wish I could.*
- *I meet friends for coffee and I enjoy it but they always stay on longer than I can. I end up being late for other commitments but I don't like to seem rude in leaving early.*
- *I always get fobbed off when I take something back to a shop or complain to customer services.*
- *I was brought up to be nice. Saying no is impolite.*
- *I always end up with extra responsibility at work, but no extra pay or promotion. I can't refuse – it may count against me.*

Insight

When you look at the list of reasons you should be assertive, it might seem a no-brainer – of course we all want some of that. But it's important to recognize what may be the perceived drawbacks – the reasons why we may not want to be assertive. Because it's often these reasons that come between us and being so.

LEARNING TO BE UNASSERTIVE

I have said that it's instinctive to react to stressful situations with fight or flight. But part of our unassertive behaviour is also learned behaviour. We learn as children and teenagers and adults to be accommodating, to give in, to avoid making waves. You have to learn this – have you ever met an accommodating baby or even toddler? Small children are naturally selfish and self-obsessed, believing themselves to be the centre of the world and unwilling to give way for anybody or anything. A parent's or carer's job is to socialize a small child – to give unconditional love but consistent boundaries, so children learn they can have their important needs met but also have to learn a certain amount of patience and self-denial.

If children have their needs met always and immediately, eventually they grow aggressive and dominating. They learn that shouting and demanding gets you what you want. But if children never have their needs met they grow submissive and self-effacing. They learn to give in, they learn helplessness, because they realize that no matter how much they want something they're never going to get it.

But the fact that this is the end result of a process of learning of course means two things. One is that you can change – you can become less submissive and more assertive, and you can also become less dominant and aggressive, and more assertive. The other is that since we often learn our behaviour from the way people act towards us, once we change ourselves, that can help to change others. You can't change someone else. But if you alter your behaviour, they may too reassess their position and move to be more in line with you.

Insight

If you become firmer and less over-accommodating to those around you, you may discover they become less demanding.

If you're finding that you would like to become more assertive but that something holds you back you may need to:

▶ *change your picture of what being an assertive person means*
▶ *recognize you don't have to lose some nice aspects of yourself*
▶ *do it slowly, over a period of time: small steps are best.*

CHANGE YOUR PICTURE OF WHAT BEING AN ASSERTIVE PERSON MEANS

Look at the pros and cons of being assertive and the pros and cons of being non-assertive, and recognize the upsides of change.

Becoming assertive isn't going to mean becoming the person you hate – it means becoming a firmer you. Being assertive isn't the same as being pushy. But we sometimes get pushy when we want to be assertive, fail... and then blow up. So being assertive is actually less pushy than aggressive. Yes, being an assertive person will mean having to make choices and take responsibility. But while being unassertive might allow you to duck the responsibility, it also means you duck the opportunities and the sense of control and achievement. And, most important, you are still making choices when you opt for unassertiveness. Not acting is a choice in itself.

RECOGNIZE YOU DON'T HAVE TO LOSE SOME NICE ASPECTS OF YOURSELF

Submissive people may also be sensitive, empathetic, kind, caring, helpful and thoughtful, while aggressive people may be dynamic, exciting, can-do, ambitious, confident and optimistic. All of these are positive qualities and you'll want to keep them. What you need to do, however, is detach them from the more negative aspects of that kind of behaviour pattern – the self-effacement and self-denial aspects of accepting everyone else goes first, and the selfish, self-interested side of being dominant. Being assertive allows you to keep the good and lose the bad.

DO IT SLOWLY, OVER A PERIOD OF TIME: SMALL STEPS ARE BEST

Nobody changes overnight. You're not going to wake up and be that totally confident assertive person tomorrow. It took time and effort to make you what you are now and it will take time and effort and mindfulness to make yourself what you'd like to be, and what you can happily manage. Don't be anxious that you're somehow going to have to jump, all of a sudden, unprepared and unskilled, into having to manage new habits and new expectations. You'll do it by small and manageable steps, a bit at a time. But step at a time, you will do it.

Jabeer told me that he had tried to become more forceful but it simply didn't work. It sounded to me as if he had felt overwhelmed with the amount of change that might be needed, and so kept trying, backtracking and feeling a failure. Expecting yourself to make enormous and instant changes just sets you up for a fall, I suggested to him. It would be far better to focus on one little area in which he could make a difference, and so make things a bit easier. Jabeer felt he had too much on his plate, and had furious arguments with his wife over seeing more of the children. So he decided to make one change; he told his work colleagues he wouldn't be joining them for a drink every Friday night because he wanted to get home to see his children. As he had feared, they teased him. But it wasn't as bad as he had expected, and the pleasure in being home in time to eat with and read bedtime stories to his kids more than made up for that. Jabeer felt himself becoming far less stressed as a result. A week or so later he noticed quite a few of his colleagues began doing the same thing, and clearly felt as relaxed as he did. Having had such a success, Jabeer now felt ready to move on to the next bit. Eventually, he discovered he'd made enormous changes, bit by bit.

Essential points to consider

1   *Stay calm and avoid 'fight or flight' when the going gets tough.*
2   *In difficult situations try to affirm calm thoughts that put you in control.*
3   *The language you use is important – how you say things matters just as much as what you say.*
4   *Consider what your reasons may be for finding it hard to become assertive.*
5   *Recognize it will take time but all you need to do is make small changes, one at a time.*

Why should you be assertive?

Why should you be assertive? Because it's pleasanter than fighting and much nicer than always giving in. Because it's more efficient than either, too. Being aggressive may appear to get you what you want in that instance. What it sets up, however, is an atmosphere in which people do not want to co-operate with you and may work hard at frustrating you. The more aggressive you are, the more aggressive you are driven to be. And the less other people enjoy your company. Being submissive is as bad. The more you let people walk all over you, they more they will take advantage – not just because it's easy to get what they want when you are going to let them, but simply because bowing your head encourages people to kick it.

Insight

Being assertive is a better way of behaving for the person being assertive and also for those around them, whether close family or friends, work colleagues, acquaintances or just the people you encounter as you go about your business.

To be assertive, however, you need to do more than simply learn a set number of tricks and strategies, tips, communication skills and behaviours. You'll find plenty of those in this book and they will prove invaluable to you in becoming a self-assured, confident and charming person to be with. What you also need is a new attitude of mind. To be assertive, you need to accept and recognize and acknowledge that you matter. You have as much right as anyone else to have what you need and want. Not more and certainly not less – but as much.

Assertiveness is, in other words, mainly an attitude of mind with an accompanying set of beliefs about yourself and the world around you. Assertiveness begins by examining the hidden beliefs we have about our worth and the worth of other people. When you have the belief that you are equal to every other person, not better or worse, you can communicate from a position of equality. And that is what you will learn and practise in later chapters.

10 THINGS TO REMEMBER

1 *Becoming assertive is a choice. It comes with responsibility attached and you will need to accept this before starting your journey.*

2 *When you start out you may meet opposition from others, but also be prepared for obstacles you may put in your own way.*

3 *Assertive behaviour includes and involves other people. It does not dominate or exclude them.*

4 *Aggression or domination will always fail on the day a bigger bully or dominator arrives on the scene.*

5 *Being passive may seem the easy way out, but it is not good for you or the people around you.*

6 *Becoming assertive does not mean a total life change – it will be the same you but one that feels better about yourself.*

7 *Remember you are trying to stand by your own feelings and beliefs and to control your choices – not to control others.*

8 *Assertiveness is not instinctive – you will need tools and strategies to help retrain yourself successfully.*

9 *You may start your journey with a particular person or circumstance in mind but, once learned, assertiveness will help you in any situation.*

10 *The main reasons for becoming assertive are that it improves your life and* **it makes you feel good!**

HOW FAR DO I HAVE TO GO?

Go through this quiz, marking each question True or Not true.

		True	Not true
1	I can accept compliments easily and sincerely.		
2	I give compliments easily and sincerely.		
3	I tend to see the good side of other people.		
4	I find it easier to criticize people than praise them.		
5	I can think of more negative characteristics of myself than I can positive.		
6	I tell people when I think they've done a good job.		
7	I get embarrassed when someone thanks me or praises me.		
8	I praise my children more often than I tell them off.		
9	It's hard for me to tell my parents how much I love them.		
10	If I get defective goods from a shop, I can return them easily.		
11	If I'm not happy with what I'm served I can send a dish back in a restaurant.		
12	I can disagree with people.		
13	If there is something I don't like about a service, I usually don't say anything to the person, but I complain to others.		
14	If a family member or a close friend is annoying me, I usually pretend not to be bothered.		

		True	Not true
15	When someone seems unhappy with me I can ask them what's wrong.		
16	I smile even when I am not happy.		
17	I find it difficult to negotiate prices for purchases, services or repairs.		
18	When people push in front of me, I usually let them.		
19	I have a hard time saying 'no'.		
20	I get involved in activities merely because someone I know asked me to.		
21	If I get invited somewhere and do not want to go, I usually make up a story and beg off.		
22	I can say sincerely to people 'No thanks, I am not interested.'		
23	I know how much I can handle and am careful not to take on too much.		
24	I think of new projects or activities and then do them.		
25	I can ask a member of the opposite sex for lunch or dinner.		
26	I feel left out because not many people invite me to join in.		
27	I easily start conversations with new people.		
28	I don't like meeting new people.		
29	I can tell people that I care about them.		

Scores

1	True 2	Not true 1		5	True 1	Not true 2
2	True 2	Not true 1		6	True 2	Not true 1
3	True 2	Not true 1		7	True 1	Not true 2
4	True 1	Not true 2		8	True 2	Not true 1

9	True 1	Not true 2		20	True 1	Not true 2	
10	True 2	Not true 1		21	True 1	Not true 2	
11	True 2	Not true 1		22	True 2	Not true 1	
12	True 2	Not true 1		23	True 2	Not true 1	
13	True 1	Not true 2		24	True 2	Not true 1	
14	True 1	Not true 2		25	True 2	Not true 1	
15	True 2	Not true 1		26	True 1	Not true 2	
16	True 1	Not true 2		27	True 2	Not true 1	
17	True 1	Not true 2		28	True 1	Not true 2	
18	True 1	Not true 2		29	True 2	Not true 1	
19	True 1	Not true 2					

How did you do?

58–45

You tend to stand up for yourself and help other people too. You are rarely aggressive and you also stand up for your rights, but are respectful of other people at the same time. You can probably see what else you have to do to be the assertive person you've always wanted to be. Read on to do even better!

44–21

You can be assertive and can use appropriate behaviours. Use the results of this quiz when reading the following chapters to see what areas you need to develop to become the assertive person you've always wanted to be.

20–29

You have some work to do. Use the results of this quiz to see what you need to do to become the assertive person you've always wanted to be. You will find all you need to boost your score in succeeding chapters.

2

The tactics we use to get along

In this chapter you will learn:

- *how to recognize your present tactic for coping*
- *about giving in, demanding, pulling strings or standing up for yourself*
- *why avoiding difficulties doesn't solve the situation*
- *about win/win solutions*
- *how to approach becoming assertive.*

What are you doing?

Most people, whether they realize it or not, tend to fall into using one of four main tactics to get by in life. You may mix and match, operating one tactic with certain people and another with others, or one in particular situations and another in different circumstances. But on the whole, we all tend to operate in a style that we've grown used to, seems to feel comfortable or appears to be the one that works best for us. Or, of course, a style that having fallen into we feel we can't get away from. We may:

- ▶ *give in*
- ▶ *demand*
- ▶ *back off but get your own way by less obvious means*
- ▶ *negotiate.*

Which do you tend to do? To work out your style, try this quiz.

It's Christmas. Do you:

1 *Have the entire family for lunch even though it's exhausting and no fun for you, because if you don't, who will?*
2 *Tell your sister you're coming round to her. She doesn't mind – she always has the family!*
3 *Say 'I'll be on my own. No, don't worry, I'll be alright. I'll put something together…'*
4 *Invite the family and get everyone to bring a dish, and give everyone a part to play in clearing up so you can all enjoy it. Say it'll be 'carriages at eight' so you can have some time just with your partner and kids in the evening.*

You're late for a meeting. Do you:

1 *Interrupt the meeting to make excuses, saying 'I know I'm late but I couldn't help it – a buyer called and I couldn't get them off the phone…'*
2 *March in and expect them to start the meeting again.*
3 *Creep in but disrupt the meeting saying 'Am I late? Oh dear, don't mind me. Can I just…? Oh dear, I'm sorry to be such a nuisance, but could we just…'*
4 *Say quietly 'Sorry I'm late. I'll catch up as we go along' and make sure you get a proper debrief afterwards.*

You come home to find a member of the family has left the kitchen in a mess. Do you:

1 *Clean up after them.*
2 *Call them in, read them the riot act and tell them if they don't clear up **now** they're in trouble for a week.*
3 *Clean up while complaining that nobody ever thinks about you, you've got so much on your plate it's not fair. If they try to make amends, shoo them away saying 'You'll only make it worse. If you want a job done well you have to do it yourself.'*
4 *Say 'I expect you to clean up after yourself. Do it now while I start making supper and we can chat.'*

You take an item that was defective when you got it home back to a shop and the assistant says they'll send it for repair at your expense. Do you:

1 *Meekly accept that's the way it is.*
2 *Shout 'How dare you! I know my rights. You'll fix it at your expense or else!'*
3 *Stand wringing your hands, saying 'Oh, I'm sure that's not right. Well, if you say so but are you sure that's all you can do?' until a crowd forms and they give you a replacement to make you go away.*
4 *Quietly, politely but firmly inform them that since the item was defective when they gave it to you, they will now give you a working replacement or a refund.*

A friend drops in out of the blue on a very busy day, says she has to go buy an outfit for an important event and as she hasn't got anyone to look after her very lively 4-year-old she's leaving him with you. Do you:

1 *Smile through gritted teeth and say 'Of course!' even though this will mess up your arrangements.*
2 *Send her packing with a flea in her ear.*
3 *Say yes but over coffee before she goes tell her all your problems so she ends up feeling so guilty she takes the child with her.*
4 *Say kindly but firmly, 'No, I won't be able to help. If you'd rung yesterday I might have been able to arrange something but I can't do it at such short notice.'*

Your mother used to ring once a day but lately it's become several times a day. Next time she calls do you:

1 *Take the call even though you feel irritated and stressed and get annoyed with her.*
2 *Tell her 'I can't talk now' and put down the phone.*
3 *Use caller display to avoid picking up the phone to her.*

4 *Say 'It's lovely talking to you once a day, Mum, but I am busy. Let me call you tomorrow at 5 when we can have a long chat. Sounds to me as if you're needing some support so let's talk about that then.'*

How did you do?
Mostly 1s? Your style is to always give in, to be submissive or passive.

Mostly 2s? You demand, or have an aggressive response.

Mostly 3s? You back off and appear to give in but then get your own way by various less obvious or hidden ways, which means you're being passive-aggressive.

Mostly 4s? Your style is to negotiate or to be assertive.

We may aspire to assertive answers but find ourselves mostly doing something else. Why do we tend to fall into other styles, and how do each of these ways of coping work for us?

How is it working?

SUBMISSIVE OR PASSIVE BEHAVIOUR

If your answers to the questions above were mostly 1s, you tend towards submissive behaviour. You do not stand up for yourself. You may express your views in a very cautious or mild manner, or you may not express them at all. You probably allow other people to push ahead of you in queues and accept that you always come second or third when sharing. You may go without new clothes or gadgets while other people in your family get what they want. Your birthday or festival present is always the one bought out of the last few pennies – or forgotten or deferred because 'Oh, don't mind me – we can't really afford anything for me!' At work or even in the family, you usually allow others to take credit for work you have done.

You may well resent being used and put upon but you're too biddable to do anything about it. Your general style is to act helpless, be indecisive and look to others to make decisions, to wail, moan and constantly apologize.

Insight

A passive person aims to get along by not rocking the boat. Their motto may be 'If it ain't broke, don't fix it', not realizing that it is broken and does need fixing. They give in, which tends to make them feel out of control and powerless, and thus aggrieved and ill-used. And as a result, the people with whom they deal are put in the position of being the dominant ones – not always a comfortable place to be in.

What happens when we take the 'easy' route by letting other people set the pace?

You don't get what you want. Submissive people often expect their partner, family or friends to 'just know' what they need and what they want. 'But I shouldn't have to say, they should know!' is a common complaint in the letters I receive as an agony aunt. You expect your boss to realize when you've done all that work and reward you. You expect your partner to know when you're feeling down and could do with some comfort. You expect your family to know when you want them to pull their weight and do their chores. And since they don't – because *no one can read minds* – you live in a constant state of disappointment, and repeatedly have to do all the extra work because everyone else is looking out for themselves, not after you.

You don't avoid confrontation. Confrontation and challenge, arguments and disagreements will still arise. What happens if you are someone who lets other people set the agenda is that you just run from it when it comes up. It's still going on, but behind your back and out of your sight. Which can mean whatever is said or resolved does so in ways that are far more of a problem to you, because you're not there to fight your corner.

Rather than avoiding clashes, you may set up situations in which unpleasantness happens more often. Since you don't challenge whatever or whoever caused the difficulty or sort out the reasons behind it, the situation or disagreement will probably reoccur, and may be far more difficult to sort out because you keep letting it escalate behind your back.

You will lose the ability to manage. The more you avoid difficult situations or people, the more you convince yourself that you're someone who cannot cope. And you will be right, because you won't learn how to resolve or face up to conflict by always running away from it. Since you don't learn or practise those skills, your ability to cope will decrease and your self-esteem and self-respect will get lower and lower. Your relationships with other people may well become more and more distant and problematical.

You will constantly be disappointed, frustrated and stressed. Instead of avoiding hassle by taking the easy path, in fact you're likely to find your life becoming more difficult. You won't have the skills to cope with any disagreements so they go on around you, continuously putting you under pressure.

Your relationships with colleagues, friends and family may also deteriorate. You may feel always letting them have their way will endear you to them and gain their approval. In fact, most people find nothing quite as frustrating as having a colleague, friend or family member who always says 'Oh, I don't know – you choose. Don't mind me – you go ahead and make the decision.' You not only make them do all the work, which is tiring and stressful, but you push them into being selfish and even into being bullies.

What are the things you might say?
You can notice if you're being submissive since you may find yourself using a lot of negative words:

'I can't...; we don't...; she won't...; you mustn't...; we oughtn't...; they shouldn't...'

So, typical submissive statements might be:

*'I'm sorry to take up your time but could you help me with this?
I know I'm being very silly but I just can't find what I'm looking for.'*

*'I can't buy myself anything new, my children need new things far
more than I do.'*

*'I'd love to have a weekend away on our own but we really shouldn't.
I'd feel terrible not taking the kids.'*

*'Would you be upset if we went out tonight? I would like to see
that film I've been waiting for but how do you feel?'*

*'Of course that's OK – whatever you want. We don't have to eat
that meal tonight – we can have it another time.'*

*'It's only my opinion but I thought it looked rather nice like that.
But of course if you don't like it we'll have it another way.'*

Why do you do it this way?
What's the pay-off of being submissive?

Insight

Pay-offs are what make us opt for one tactic or other. It's
what we get out of the situation and often, pay-offs can mean
something entirely different to different people. Sometimes,
people choose pay-offs that appear to be negative but in fact
suit their needs.

Short-term pay-offs of being passive
In the short term you:

Avoid conflict. A pay-off for letting other people have their way
and sidelining our own is that we avoid arguments. Being passive
and submissive can feel like a very simple and effortless route.
You can honestly boast that you and your family, your friends,
your colleagues, never have a cross word or a disagreement, and

that can seem encouraging. Another pay-off of staying quiet about your needs or wishes may also be that you can feel downtrodden and abused. Many people would see that as undesirable. In fact, you can find a certain satisfaction in it – at least it's a predictable outcome. If you look for and work towards the positive result of being heard, you might feel that for all that hard work you only get a percentage of times that your effort is rewarded. If you never try, one advantage is that you get exactly what you expect – 100 per cent hit rate on being right and getting nothing. It can seem easier to play the martyr than to take steps to be heard.

Avoid taking responsibility. By avoiding taking responsibility, you can rest comfortably in the knowledge that you'll never be called to account, never be blamed, never have to explain yourself because it's never your fault. Taking the back position can seem a very safe place to be.

Long term pay-offs of being passive
The long term pay-offs of being passive and submissive can be less acceptable. While the immediate pay-offs can seem comfortable, protecting you from conflict and accountability, in the long run it can become distressing.

In the long term you:

Lose even more self-esteem, confidence and worth. The more you avoid conflict, the scarier raised voices, disagreements and anger become. Your tolerance for conflict may go down so even the slightest difference can make you panic. The more you avoid it, the less able you feel you are in managing or resolving any such clash – your self-esteem, your confidence and your feelings of self-worth may consequently reduce. And it's not just in dealing with rows you may lose self-confidence – you may come to see yourself as someone who simply 'can't manage' in many areas.

Build resentment. You may find yourself becoming more resentful of the people you lean on. Since their choices may not be to your advantage, or taste, you may increasingly lose patience with their always taking charge. And they may resent you. Even in a partnership or a family, you might be seen as a freeloader or a drag – someone who gains from the hard work they do without doing your bit. You may not realize or notice all the efforts other people have to make to cover for you.

Suffer stress-related medical problems. People who constantly put themselves at the back of the queue may also find that always giving way, even if you're scared or unused to doing anything else, can become wearing. You may find panic attacks and other stress-related difficulties can develop and increase the more you duck your head and hide behind others.

How does it affect those around you?
How does always being submissive affect the people around you? Other people may react by:

▶ *being sorry for you*
▶ *looking down on you*
▶ *taking advantage of you*
▶ *avoiding you.*

Being sorry for you. It may seem pleasant to have sympathy. It gets less pleasant when people are sorry for what you are rather than for a specific situation. Being sorry *for* you quickly becomes being sorry *about* you.

Looking down on you. Once they've felt sorry for you, people – even your nearest and dearest – may soon start to make judgements on how much your difficulties are down to your own actions. Instead of feeling sympathy for having a tough time and being pushed around, they may begin to feel condescension or contempt. Being submissive may be seen as being agreeable or wanting to avoid arguments. It can also be seen in a far less sympathetic light, as not making an effort and taking an easy route.

Taking advantage of you. If you're kind and gentle and never make waves, people pretty soon catch on to the fact that you'll always say yes and never say no. It's like walking around with a sign saying 'Kick me!' on your back. Sadly, all too many people will do exactly that. Or, in the case of the endlessly obliging, endlessly require them to oblige.

Avoiding you. Submissive people may be agreeable but sooner or later they can become discomforting. By always agreeing, never confronting, you present a challenge, because other people have to look after you or be responsible for you or suffer you hanging on giving nothing back. It can become wearisome – and for that reason, they may begin to avoid you or leave you out of arrangements. It's not that they've forgotten to include you because you don't make waves, it's that they've consciously excluded you for that reason.

Essential points to consider

1 *Most of us tend towards one or other style, giving in or demanding, backing off or pulling strings, or simply being assertive.*
2 *It's worthwhile recognizing the short- and long-term pay-offs to your usual style.*
3 *What you do to get by at present may seem easy but have hidden drawbacks.*

AGGRESSIVE BEHAVIOUR

If your answers to the questions above were mostly 2s, you lean towards aggressive behaviour. Aggressive behaviour tends to show little or no concern for other people's ideas, feelings and needs. If you are being aggressive your actions may be bossy and arrogant, and help you get your way by bulldozing others. Aggression goes with being intolerant, opinionated and overbearing. An aggressive person gets along by insisting on their rights using anger, threats and sometimes even open violence to be on top. If you tend towards being aggressive you may feel strong and in control, and nod towards the fact that you make the choices and call the shots to justify your behaviour. You may not get many spontaneous presents from other people but you make absolutely sure you're first in line when anything is being handed out, and that nobody is in any doubt what you expect them to get you on the right occasions.

You may be happy with your actions, or at least feel justified by the results in using this behaviour. Your general style is to be in control, decisive, and to raise your voice so everyone hears what you want, what you think and what you expect.

Insight

An aggressive person aims to get along by always being up front and in the lead. Their motto might be 'Nobody is going to get one over me – I know best'. Constant aggression is exhausting and depressing and leaves the aggressor feeling continually under threat themselves, and so inclined to increase their demands and attempts to be in front. Those around them feel intimidated and afraid, and often harbour simmering anger and hatred and little respect for them.

What happens when we take the route of always setting ourselves above and in front of other people?
You get what you insist on. However, it may not always be what you need or even want. By setting the pace you deny those around you the chance to think for themselves and to co-operate with you and between themselves. Aggression stifles innovation – everyone is too busy trying to follow instructions and please the aggressor to have time to think around the issues and come up with their own ideas.

You live in a state of frequent confrontation. Telling people what to do, refusing to listen to their points of view, means you constantly have to assert yourself and your position, and take steps to make sure other people do not win over you. Aggression tends to be met with aggression, so you spend much of your time going up against other people and beating them down. One fight tends to lead to another since aggression does not solve problems, it simply steamrollers over opponents on each occasion, leaving new problems to arise, or the same problem to come up when the other person feels able to try again.

You limit your ability to learn and to develop. Since aggression appears to work, people who use it tend not to learn other strategies – negotiation, compromise, discussion and consensus. This prevents both the aggressor and those around them learning and developing those skills and any other new approaches. Sooner or later they may run out of steam or meet a bigger and more aggressive opponent, and then find they are stuck.

You put yourself under enormous stress. Constantly having the 'fight' button on is exhausting and no matter how much adrenaline and arrogance pushes you forward, the effort needed to maintain this behaviour can have damaging effects on emotional and physical health.

Your relationships with colleagues, friends and family may be unsympathetic. However much such behaviour is apparently admired in business circles as being 'can-do' and effective, in fact it has severe limitations. With family and friends it is not only ineffective but harmful. People may tolerate you but not love you, live with you but not accept you, respect you but not like you. And in fact, in society at large the 'respect for a strong personality' is beginning to give way to dislike of a bully.

What are the things you might say?
You can notice if you're being aggressive if you:

- ▶ *use sarcasm*
- ▶ *put the blame for problems and mistakes on someone else*
- ▶ *shout, swear, use abusive language*
- ▶ *resort to physical displays – pushing, shoving, slapping.*

So, typical aggressive statements might be:

'Spaghetti? I don't want that bilge – give me a cottage pie tonight.'

'Oh, that's really clever, isn't it? Oh yes, that was brilliant – I don't think.'

'Don't ask questions – do what I've told you.'

'That's just about the stupidest idea I've heard all week.'

'Just get out of my way and let me do it…'

'You stupid idiot! What the **** do you think you're doing?'

'It's nothing to do with me – it's all your fault.'

What's the short-term pay-off of being aggressive?
The pay-offs for being aggressive seem pretty obvious. In the short
term you:

Have a sense of power. By being aggressive, you are the top of the
tree and are in control. Nobody pushes you around, nobody makes
you do anything you don't want to do and everybody does what you
choose. You might feel that any dissent and disagreement in your
family and at work are minimized because you know best and lay
down the rules. In fact, you may feel justified in that by putting down
your foot, arguments seem to be held at bay, since if you're aggressive
enough, nobody answers back and all seems peaceful.

Get what you want. People who use aggression are confident that
they have their needs fulfilled, and that they can also help other
people to avoid wasting time and effort in dithering and time-
consuming discussion by getting straight to the point and doing
what they have decided.

Take the lead and get the credit. Using aggression usually means
that when things work out you can claim the glory. Of course,
being on top also means if things go wrong you can also point the
finger at someone else and make it their fault, not yours.

What's the long-term pay-off of being aggressive?
The long-term pay-offs of being aggressive can be less acceptable.
While the immediate pay-offs can seem comfortable, putting you

in control, in the long run it can become distressing. In the long term you:

Need to maintain a constant level of stress and pressure. Living with daily conflict can give you a tolerance for it, so that anger and fighting seem normal. You and all around you may assume that a raised voice is always the way to settle any disagreement. You may lose or never develop the skills of discussion, negotiation and compromise, or simply forget to use or apply them.

Increase loneliness. Using aggression usually means you're on your own, making decisions and choices. It's not a co-operative style, which means you may feel resentful at having to be the only one bearing all the responsibility.

Suffer stress-related medical problems. People who constantly put themselves on alert to fight may find it becomes exhausting. Stress-related difficulties can develop and increase the more you push yourself forward and others back.

Rely on being forceful to feel self-esteem, self-confidence and self-worth. When something happens to interrupt the established order, someone who uses aggression may find it hard to maintain their positive feelings about themselves.

How does it affect those around you?
How does always being aggressive affect the people around you? Other people react by:

- *being aggressive back*
- *disliking you and not trusting you*
- *avoiding you.*

Being aggressive back. Anger, blame and threat tend to be met by the same. Be aggressive enough and most people will back off. But some will fight, so people being aggressive tend to find themselves always having to step into the ring. They may feel that's because the world is full of people challenging them; it's more likely that the world is full of people reacting to them. Aggression leads to aggression that leads to more aggression – it's an unending cycle.

Disliking you and not trusting you. Even the people who don't fight back are hardly likely to welcome aggressive behaviour. Contrary to the beliefs sometimes held by those who use it, aggression isn't seen as decisive, forceful, dynamic or in any other positive light. It's seen as bullying, overwhelming, frightening, unfair. When aggression is used, family, friends and colleagues may do what they are told but they may also react with suppressed anger, disgust, dislike. They may not trust the person being aggressive and do their best to frustrate them but in stealthy ways.

Avoiding you. Nobody likes to be pushed around. Whether it's by a friend or family member, a work colleague or simply someone you bump into in the street, aggression tends to lead to people going out of their way not to be in the company of someone using it. You may think this a wonderful bonus if it gets you a seat in the train or first place in a queue. It's less fun when your friends avoid you and don't invite you to some events; when your family would rather be in another room or eat meals together before you come home; and when colleagues sharing lunch, coffee or a chat melt away when you come near them.

Case study

Bella told her husband Dan she wanted a divorce but was willing to give him one last chance if he agreed to counselling. When I saw them she pointed out she had asked him to talk over their difficulties many times during their ten years together and she was angry he would only finally agree as a last resort. Dan saw himself as a good provider to her and their children – he worked in the City, where his forceful manner and decisiveness made him very successful. He was proud of his achievements and reluctant to change what he saw as a winning formula. She said being a success in their relationship and with their children was a bit more complex and she'd have liked to see him keeping his promises to

(Contd)

take them out over weekends, share evening meals together and be there for their school parent nights, sports days and plays. Dan saw his behaviour as vital, macho and desirable – he was looked up to as a mover and shaker at work. Bella saw it differently. 'When one of our children was having a tough time at school, all Dan could do was shout at him and tell him not to be such a wimp. And when our relationship started going downhill, all he could do was run off to work. I don't think he wants to change because he can't see that anything needs to be different.' Dan saw Bella's behaviour as a bluff – as far as he was concerned, it was like arguing over a contract with a client. It wasn't until Bella moved out of the house, moving three hundred miles to stay with her parents and began making arrangements for the children to attend school there that he recognized what he stood to lose. Dan had to make a choice of three options. He had to change his style altogether, to separate how he managed his family life and his work life, or lose his wife and children. He decided the last was not what he wanted but the first may be too hard. With Bella's help, Dan worked very hard at becoming assertive rather than aggressive, at least at home.

PASSIVE-AGGRESSIVE BEHAVIOUR

If your answers to the questions above were mostly 3s, you tend towards passive-aggressive behaviour. Passive-aggressive behaviour tends to be exhibited by those who want their own way but are too low in self-confidence or self-worth to demand it assertively, or aggressively. But that doesn't mean it's any less powerful than out-and-out aggression. Passive-aggressive behaviour may be sarcastic, deceptive and ambiguous, is manipulative and works by making others feel guilt or shame and so giving the user what they want. Someone may use passive-aggression, not to push their way to the front of the queue, but wander there as if they hadn't noticed there was a queue. Or to sigh and softly complain until you usher them in front of you, or are left feeling ashamed that you were so unreasonable. Passive-aggressive behaviour works by its user being calculating and controlling, and making other people feel embarrassed and bamboozled into doing what the user wants.

Someone using passive-aggression may say nothing ever goes their way and that they are ignored and passed over. They may say one thing, do another, and then deny ever saying the first thing. They don't communicate their needs and wishes in a clear manner, expecting family, friends and colleagues to read their mind and meet their needs. Indeed, they'll actively withhold information about how they feel because they may be scared that if you knew what they were thinking or feeling you'd criticize them.

People who use passive-aggression may say they would love things to be different – but frustrate any support or suggestions towards change. One reason is that they lack trust in others and have such a negative and passive outlook. The other is that they get what they want far more often than anyone realizes. Their effect on other people, however, is profound. Using complaints and reproaches, sabotage and indirect criticism results in the person using passive-aggression getting their own way but at the cost of sowing guilt and discord.

What happens when we use passive-aggression?
What happens when we use manipulation and indirect strategies in our dealings with friends, family, colleagues and others?

Sometimes you do and sometimes you don't get what you want.
Using manipulation and behind the scenes moves to try and direct affairs your own way can be surprisingly effective and those using passive-aggression succeed far more often than you might think. However, their behaviour frequently leaves everyone feeling awful. They feel bad because they are convinced by their own complaints and excuses that they are having a poor deal. Everyone else may feel guilty or ashamed, annoyed or impatient. The user and the used tend to feel stressed and unhappy.

You avoid outright confrontation. Passive-aggression tends more to niggling arguments in the background about how unfair it is or how nothing goes right but rarely results in obvious quarrels.

However, the effect on everyone can be far more distressing and tiring than falling out. This is because in a shouting match you may resolve matters – at least things are out in the open. With passive-aggression, it continues in the background, is persistent, hard to resolve and often denied.

You'll feel negative and defensive. Passive-aggressive behaviour works by the person using it believing they are hard done by, and manoeuvring everyone else to believe so as well. It takes effort to convince yourself you are forever on the back foot, and stress and pressure tends to discourage the user from ever trying other strategies – from trying to be positive and proactive.

You'll be trapped in 'learned helplessness'. While passive-aggressive behaviour can be displayed by insisting on doing work instead of delegating – 'Don't bother, I'll do it!' – it also often results in the user claiming they are ineffectual and incompetent. And the more you tell other people, and yourself, you can't do it, the more that becomes a self-fulfilling prophecy. Just as we can learn to do things, we can be taught and teach ourselves to be unable: that's 'learned helplessness'.

You will be stuck. By never communicating your needs or asking for other people's you may miss the fact that you could get a lot of what you want in far less destructive ways. Passive-aggressive behaviour is inefficient and delays any resolution of a problem.

People using passive-aggressive behaviour tend to come across as stubborn and sullen, and colleagues, friends and family may find it hard to sympathize or co-operate with someone using it. People may make allowances and adjust to let someone who uses this make the running, but they also may eventually withdraw. Either because they realize what is happening and refuse to play that game anymore. Or simply because being manipulated is unpleasant and frustrating and they vote with their feet not to have it happen any more.

You can notice if you're being passive-aggressive since you may:

▶ *be persistently late for appointments and often forget or delay doing tasks that are your responsibility*

- ▶ *blame everyone or everything but yourself when things go wrong*
- ▶ *complain of being misunderstood and unappreciated*
- ▶ *rarely mean what you say or say what you mean*
- ▶ *never lose your temper.*

What are the things you might say?

'*It's not my fault!*'

'*It's all very well for you!*'

'*No, I'm fine. I'm not angry, really. It's alright – I'm perfectly happy…*'

'*I was going to do it but then…*'

'*Nobody ever listens to a word I say…*'

'*You're always getting at me!*'

'*You can't trust anyone.*'

'*Oh, leave that. I'll clear up after you – if you want a job done properly, you have to do it yourself.*'

What's the short-term pay-off of being passive-aggressive?
In the short term you:

Feel safe. People who use passive-aggression usually come from families in which honest expression of feelings was forbidden. This tends to teach children to repress and deny their feelings and to use other means to express their frustration or anger and get their needs met. Manipulating those around them and denying their own feelings and needs makes them feel in control and protected.

Get what you want. You won't ask for what you want or express your real feelings to get what you need, but somehow you end up avoiding doing stuff you don't want to do and having people fall in with your schemes, in spite of themselves.

Keep out of the line of fire. By often neglecting your responsibilities you may get criticized for not doing as much as you should, but you also avoid being held to task. And by leading from behind, by getting people to do what you want by manipulation and suggestion, you can always blame the people who appeared to be in the lead if it goes wrong.

Play the victim. You can gather great sympathy and support from people who don't know you very well by always framing events in your favour. You'd love to see your friends and family – they abandon you by not being in touch. You'd love to take a leading role at work – they neglect your skills by passing you by. Your life would be fine – if only people in authority didn't have it in for you.

What's the long-term pay-off of being passive-aggressive?
The long-term pay-offs of being passive-aggressive can be less acceptable. While the immediate pay-offs can seem comfortable, making people sorry for you and protecting you from accountability, in the long run it can become distressing. In the long term you:

Are always on the edge. Using passive-aggression takes a lot of energy and work, all aimed at blaming others for shortcomings and ducking out of responsibilities. You may spend a lot of time feeling victimized, being unable to trust others, feeling sulky and resentful. Always being late and resisting the things you should be doing at work, at home and with friends, takes more out of you than getting on and doing them.

Build your self-esteem, self-worth and self-confidence on shaky foundations. If you convince yourself that it's never your fault but always other people's, that you are hard done by and it's only bad luck that holds you back, you risk one day discovering that it's actually down to you. You may need to work hard to continue to convince yourself it's everyone else's fault. And, of course, you never have the chance to be in control of your own self-esteem.

Are alone. Passive-aggressive behaviour tends to go hand in hand with a distrust of authority and a fear of being close to people – either of having to step up and be compared, or of relying on them.

Can be stuck and at a loss. Passive-aggression is about steering clear of anger – about having been taught, as a child, that anger is unacceptable. But we all feel anger – it's how we deal with it that matters. Most children learn to cope with negative feelings – to accept them, work with them and manage them. If what you have learned is to bury anger and hostility you never grow beyond it – anger is constantly under the surface and you can't gain the skills to deal with it. What people with passive-aggressive behaviour are doing is dealing with feelings like a toddler and either being overwhelmed by them or hiding from them. This might be acceptable and understandable behaviour in a young child, but highly dysfunctional in an adult.

Suffer stress-related medical problems. Constantly suppressing anger is not good for your health. It tends to come out in health issues for the person suppressing it, and in less obvious ways for everyone around them. People suppressing anger tend to let it leak out in less open but even more destructive behaviour – sarcasm, criticism, sullenness, complaints.

How does it affect those around you?
How does always being passive-aggressive affect the people around you? Other people may react by:

▶ *initially, feeling sorry for you and guilty about you*
▶ *after a time, feeling angry, frustrated, exasperated*
▶ *becoming distant and disconnected*
▶ *giving up on you.*

Initially, feeling sorry for you and guilty about you. The family, friends and colleagues of people using passive-aggression can easily get sucked into their self-image of being the well meaning but forgetful victims of persistent personal misfortune. Those around them may get used to making allowances, covering up and doing work instead while hearing a stream of envy, complaint and criticism directed at everyone else.

Family, friends and colleagues may themselves feel insecure and apologetic while trying – vainly – to make up for all the things that the passive-aggressive person tells them are a hindrance to them.

After a time, feeling angry, frustrated, exasperated. Some family, friends and colleagues may continue to be caught up in the belief that the person using passive-aggression is a victim and if they only made the effort, filled in the gaps, it would be resolved. Some, however, are likely to realize they are being used. The person using passive-aggression may not be able to face up to anger, and may impose that reluctance on those around them, but anger will be present and may well come out with frustration and exasperation at the underhand tactics being used.

Becoming distant and disconnected. An inability to be close and intimate is part of passive-aggressive behaviour. While nearest and dearest may make efforts to bridge the gap, eventually those around them may simply give up and back off.

Giving up on you. And when they've really backed off, they may have entirely given up. Dealing with someone who uses passive-aggression can be frustrating in the extreme because they can be so submerged in their own explanation for what they do and how correct it is. Family, friends and colleagues can make efforts to show how destructive the behaviour is; the passive-aggressive will in effect respond with 'But it's all your fault – you change!' Eventually, they may simply give up.

Here, for instance, is the perfect description of a work project as run by someone who tends towards passive-aggression.

The six phases of a project:

1 *Enthusiasm.*
2 *Disillusionment.*
3 *Panic.*
4 *Search for the guilty.*

5 *Punishment of the innocent.*
6 *Praise and honours for the non-participants.*

Essential points to consider

1 *Passivity, passive-aggression or aggression might seem to provide instant rewards and results. The key is recognizing the short and long term effects of such behaviour on you and those around you.*
2 *What can seem to be a positive pay-off may have drawbacks. It might be nice to have people sorry for you, until you realize they are also sorry about you.*

ASSERTIVE BEHAVIOUR

If your answers to the questions above were mostly 4s, you tend towards assertive behaviour. If your behaviour is assertive you stand up for yourself and your rights, but you do not do so at the expense of others. You express your ideas, feelings and needs, while at the same time recognizing that other people also have the right to express and pursue their own. You may allow other people in front of you in the queue, when you're not in a hurry and someone else is. When it matters, you will firmly but quietly take a stand. Assertive people are direct and honest. They accept other people for what they are, take responsibility for their own actions but not for other people's, and are flexible and spontaneous.

Being assertive means being able to put your foot down firmly while not trampling on other people's rights. Assertive behaviour negotiates and reaches workable compromises. Assertive people have confidence in themselves and are positive, while at the same time understanding other people's points of view.

WHAT HAPPENS WHEN YOU ARE ASSERTIVE?

You don't always get what you want. Assertive people are clear about what they want and need, think and feel. They don't expect anyone – partner or family, friends or colleagues – to be able to read their minds so they say what they mean and mean what they say. At work, they will take responsibility and own up to mistakes but equally will claim credit for what they have done. Since they will also listen to other people and their needs and wants, this doesn't always mean getting what they want completely and every time – sometimes a compromise is necessary. It means, however, that they will always feel they have heard and been heard and so feel satisfied and fulfilled, knowing their needs are being mostly met.

You avoid confrontation. That does not mean you avoid challenge. Assertive people will discuss and face up to contrary views but they will do it in the spirit of co-operation, with negotiation and compromise. This means it is not an argument but an arbitration, where all views are given weight and respected. An assertive person may still say 'I'm the boss/I'm the parent and the buck stops with me', but they will do it having taken other ideas on board. By helping other people to feel respected and listened to, assertive behaviour counteracts the need for confrontation.

You feel skilled. Assertive behaviour takes some practice and takes some effort to apply but it leaves you and all around you feeling satisfied and in control.

It works! Using assertive behaviour is slower than using aggression, where you get what you want at once without debate, or submission, where you give in. It saves time in the long run, however, since assertive behaviour leaves everyone feeling OK about the situation and so more co-operative, and that tends to be far more effective.

Your relationships with family, friends and colleagues benefit. Using assertive behaviour results in everyone having their say and being heard. It may not mean you always get what you want, nor give all those around you exactly what they want every time. What it does mean is that all of you get much of what you need most of the time, and that leads to everyone feeling content.

What are the things you might say?
You know you're being assertive when you make the effort to use plenty of positive statements:

'I can...; I do...; I will...; I could...; I would...; I want...'

Typical assertive statements might be:

'I believe this... what do you think?'

'What we're going to do is...'

'Tell me how you feel about this, I'll tell you how I feel and we'll come to some agreement...'

'I want...'

'There are two differing views on this – how are we going to sort this out?'

'I would like you to...'

'What can we do to resolve this problem?'

What's the pay-off of being assertive?
In the short term you:

Build self-confidence, self-worth and self-esteem. Being assertive 'adds value'; it makes you feel good about the way you are treating other people, and does the same for them.

Move from win/lose to win/win. When you are assertive you don't always get exactly what you want when you want it, so you don't always win outright. However, your behaviour doesn't force other people into being either winners or losers either. Assertive behaviour leads to everyone sharing and compromising so that you all get some of what you want at some point, thus making you all winners in the end.

Take responsibility and feel good about it. Taking responsibility means sometimes having to shoulder the blame when things go wrong. But it also means being in the forefront with achievements.

Avoid conflict. Being assertive often means having to face up to disagreements and differences. But by dealing with them with confidence and skill, they become discussions rather than descending into quarrels.

In the long term you:

Hone more skills. Being assertive means using all sorts of skills to make your point and listen to those of others. The more you use such skills, the more of them you learn and perfect. Assertiveness skills are also 'transferable' – you can use them with family, friends, colleagues and in the world at large.

Become more effective in relationships, family and work. Being assertive fosters strong and mutually respectful relationships with those around you. Assertive behaviour allows all of you to make feelings known, feel heard by and listen to other people, have your needs met and help meet the needs of the people with whom you interact.

How does always being assertive affect others?

How does always being assertive affect the people around you? Other people may react by:

Listening to you. Being assertive means being able to clearly explain your feelings and ask for the things you want and need. You may still disagree and you may not get all you desire, but you do have the satisfaction of knowing people hear you.

Respecting and liking you. Being assertive always means having to say you are sorry, and thank you, and please. Assertive behaviour is mutual and fosters good feelings in both the assertive person and those with whom they deal. Other people may not always get what they want from you but since they will feel their needs are considered and given weight, they will respect you for using assertiveness.

Wanting to be with you. Someone who is assertive may sometimes be challenging, as they will put their own point of view and state their needs clearly, but you know where you stand with them. You also know whatever happens will be after due consideration of everyone's wishes, desires and needs and will be fair. For that reason, the company of an assertive person is desirable.

Modelling themselves on you. Once they have benefited from assertiveness skills, most people will see how effective they are and how pleasant it can be to apply them, and so will want to copy those skills and share in the effects.

In any encounter with other people, we have the option of being active – taking the conversation to them and making a contribution – or of being passive – simply letting them make the running. We also have the option of being destructive or constructive – putting them down or being judgemental and unhelpful, or being enabling and positive. Imagine a friend comes up to you and says 'We're having a baby!' Which of these answers is:

1 *passive constructive*
2 *active destructive*

3   *passive destructive*
4   *active constructive*

'*Brilliant! I always thought you two would be such good parents. When I saw the way you handled that argument last week it felt as if you'd manage bringing up a child with such confidence and kindness. How do you feel? What are your plans?*'

'*How wonderful!*'

'*Oh dear me – all those sleepless nights and children are such a drain on your purse and are always a worry....*'

'*Oh. Did I tell you my news...?*'

Which would you rather hear – and say?

(It's 4, 1, 2 and 3.)

Win/win or win/lose?

Another way of understanding the tactics we use to get along is to see them in terms of whether you win or lose. Whether you give in or demand (be submissive/passive or aggressive) the result will be that you are in a win/lose situation – one of you wins, one of you loses. The four styles we've already looked at – submissive, aggressive, passive-aggressive and assertive – can also be seen in terms of win/win or win/lose scenarios when interacting with other people. In this diagram, depending on whether you submit, use aggression, passive-aggression or assertiveness, one or both of you wins or loses.

You win! You get what you want.	I give in.	We negotiate.
You lose! You don't get what you want.	We back away.	I demand.
	I lose! I don't get what I want.	*I win! I get what I want.*

- *When I give in, you win and I lose.*
- *When I demand, I win and you lose.*
- *When we back away, we both lose.*
- *When we negotiate, we both win.*

If winning or losing feels important to you, it's easy to see how, on paper, you can get the idea that an aggressive or demanding style pays dividends and a submissive or even assertive one does not. However, even when you 'win', the end result may be unsatisfactory because it breeds resentment and ill-feeling. Being submissive, aggressive or passive-aggressive can be an uncomfortable life stance. What this book is about is exploring the win/win by using negotiation and assertiveness. You may not always get what you want, but you are in control.

Insight

What happens when we're not assertive is that we tend to be passive, or aggressive, or manipulative. We nag, we make others feel guilty or ashamed or under pressure, we threaten, we withdraw. It's a bit like having a parcel of misery: we keep it, share it or land it on others rather than unpicking and unpacking it and making it go away.

At the moment, you probably use a style other than assertive much of the time and would prefer to change. However, aspects of all four styles are tactics that can be appropriate in different circumstances. While negotiating may be the best one at most times, the other tactics are useful if not necessary in particular circumstances. One of the skills of being assertive is to know what tactic to use, when.

For example, it can be appropriate in the middle of a negotiation to back away, in order to collect your thoughts or reflect on the progress so far. Sometimes it might be more effective to make subtle suggestions rather than direct requests. And sometimes you may decide to give in simply because you want to choose your battles and only spend time on those issues that are worth the time and effort. However, if you come across a person having a heart attack in the street, it would be inappropriate to negotiate whether someone should call for an ambulance – the correct option might be to order a bystander to do it.

But if you are using these tactics inappropriately, either at the cost of effectiveness or of your own self-esteem and confidence, they may have become a habit or life stance – you may have settled into using a particular tactic as the first, or even only, choice.

Life stance

You win! You get what you want.	Submissive	Assertive
You lose! You don't get what you want.	Passive-Aggressive	Aggressive
	I lose! I don't get what I want.	I win! I get what I want.

Essential points to consider

1 *Assertiveness is standing up for yourself and your beliefs but not at the expense of others.*
2 *Assertiveness works. It may be slower than aggression or other methods, but it's far more effective.*
3 *Once you begin to assert yourself, you will get the bonus of finding that other people will start to model themselves on you.*
4 *Using negotiation produces a win/win situation, where both parties leave happy with the result.*

Child, parent, adult

Psychoanalyst Eric Berne had a helpful theory about the way we operate. He said that we have three basic selves. We're either behaving and feeling and thinking as a parent, an adult or a child. We move between these states, and we act out these roles even if we are in fact not parents nor still a child.

CHILD

When we're being a child, we may be operating from pure feeling. The child state is that of the infant, who doesn't understand and simply reacts to what is going on in an emotional, instinctive and selfish way. In child state you expect to be looked after, to be told what to do, to have your needs fulfilled by other people. But children are also fun, playful and creative. It's the child in you that suddenly decides to run barefoot through the grass – something we should all do sometimes.

PARENT

When we're being a parent, we follow the model we have picked up from the adults in our childhood. We'll try to look after, guide and control other people's behaviour – usually out of the best of intentions, as a caring mum or dad would do. Or, we may be doing it to manipulate to our own advantage, either deliberately or without realizing it. Parents take on responsibility, tell people off, take command and assume they know best. It's the parent in you who takes control when all is chaos and a decision needs to be made.

ADULT

When we're being an adult, we'll be thinking about what we're doing. Adults negotiate and communicate and instead of following patterns laid down in childhood may be going on what they've observed and worked out from personal experience. Adults are serious but try to listen and balance what is going on. It's the adult in you who offers to compromise and come to a sensible agreement.

SWITCHING THE ROLES

We can switch between the different states because either something in what is happening around us, or how we are reacting to our memories or situation, calls out each role. Or, we can fall into one role in response to the behaviour of someone else. When a work colleague acts bossily and parentally, you may find yourself becoming sulky and contrary – the child to their parent. When your partner leans on you or avoids taking a grown-up decision, you may find yourself pulled into being parental with them, not only taking control but being impatient and frustrated as you might with a recalcitrant child. And the more parental you become, the more they become the child. When you're feeling in control of yourself and the situation, you are likely to be in your adult persona. And when you act like an adult to someone else, or someone acts like an adult to you, the response is usually to be adult and calm, sensible and co-operative.

We all act out these roles to some degree and in some times and places. Indeed, we need to have varying bits of parent, child and adult in our make-up. Sometimes we have to summon up our internal parent and direct everyone to do the right thing. Without the child, we may not be able to be spontaneous and light-hearted and leave the ironing to go out and play. However grown-up you are there will be times when you want to throw it all to the winds and go play in the snow. There will always be times when we want to lean on someone else and be looked after, claiming the luxury of not having to decide. And then there will be times when it's not just appropriate but satisfying to be measured and sensible and, when we choose, to be the grown-up and in control.

Case study

Gina couldn't understand why every Christmas ended in a terrible argument between her and her sister, Carol. 'We love each other yet every time we meet up at our parents' house for Christmas, one or other of us is bound to lose it. Last year we were squabbling over something or other and it just ruined the whole thing. Yet we can see each other times – she comes to us or we go and see her – and it's fine.' I asked Gina to imagine herself back in the house at the last Christmas and to remember the quarrel and to think what it reminded her of. 'Oh,' she said immediately, 'it's just like when I was 10 and she was 12 and we used to fight over which one of us got the best present. She was always our Dad's favourite but she said I was our Mum's.' Gina realized she and her sister were simply rerunning old rows, and that their parents weren't exactly innocent bystanders. I invited her to wonder why they may not object to what was happening. 'Well, it tends to mean our husbands, and the children, become surplus to requirements. It's as if the four of us are involved and no one else. It's just like when we were young and they were in control!' Gina later told me that she and her sister talked it through and now that they could see the dynamics, were able to resist. The following Christmas might have left her parents feeling they'd lost the initiative, but the rest of the family were far happier at the proceedings.

WHEN BEING CHILD, PARENT OR ADULT CAN GO WRONG

Where these roles or states of child, adult and parent become destructive is when we get stuck in one or other exclusively or inappropriately. It might be fun to say to your partner, 'I'm not in the mood to be a big grown up today – you take over', or 'It's my turn to be the one in charge – you put your feet up and let me lead', or 'We'll have a play day today, all of us!' That's all very fine and well, until bills have to be paid, children given boundaries and decisions made. Then, the adult has to come out and you need to carefully manage your use of parent and child mode to fit the purpose.

Knowing how it works, recognizing which part of you is to the fore at the moment and how it's impacting on those around you – family, friends and colleagues – means you can manage your inner child, parent and adult in the best possible way. And it means you can also notice when other people are falling into their child/parent/ adult modes, and act accordingly. When a colleague becomes all parental on you, it only pulls your strings if you respond by acting as a child. Behave as an adult and the deliberate or unconscious attempt to make you act as a child and be dominated falls to pieces. When a family member acts the child and you find yourself either falling into childhood patterns as well or becoming parental, by realizing this you can choose to act more beneficially.

EXERCISE

Thinking of the four styles of behaviour – giving in (or being submissive), demanding (or being aggressive), backing away (or being passive-aggressive) and negotiating (or being assertive) – answer these questions to think about how you use them at present, and consider why.

Think of some examples of situations when it might be best or most appropriate to use each of these tactics – think of two scenarios for each:

Give in		
Demand		
Back away		
Negotiate		

Can you and do you use all or some of these tactics? Think of two situations when you have behaved in this way:

Give in		
Demand		

Back away		
Negotiate		

How did you feel when you used these tactics?

Give in		
Demand		
Back away		
Negotiate		

Now write down how it felt when someone else used these tactics with you. What was your reaction and feelings?

Give in		
Demand		

(Contd)

Back away		
Negotiate		

Which of the four styles do you tend to use more than others? Put them in order, and give your reasons for using each.

Give in		
Demand		
Back away		
Negotiate		

Which of the four styles might you find difficult to use? Put them in order and give your reasons for finding it difficult to use each.

Give in		
Demand		

Back away		
Negotiate		

Look at the answers you have given. Thinking of what we have discussed in this chapter, can you see some areas that need work? Put the results aside and refer back to them as we continue.

10 THINGS TO REMEMBER

1 *Before you begin practising assertiveness it's helpful to consider your coping techniques at the moment and see what you might want to change.*

2 *Being submissive and not 'rocking the boat' is not the easy route in life. Mostly it means you are frustrated, disappointed and seldom get the things you want or need.*

3 *The more you avoid difficult people and situations, the more you will convince yourself that you cannot cope with your life.*

4 *Submissiveness often has short-term gains like avoiding confrontation, conflict or responsibility, but in the long term it can produce disappointment and the loss of more self-respect and confidence.*

5 *Constant aggression might get instant results and control, but can leave the aggressor feeling exhausted, depressed and under threat themselves.*

6 *'Passive-aggression' is used by those who want their own way but lack the self-confidence to achieve it. It works by manipulating people and is as damaging to yourself and others as bullying.*

7 *Using passive-aggression long term means that you would spend more time and effort blaming others and ducking out of responsibility than you would if you faced life on a more assertive level.*

8 *Being assertive means taking control and being able to put your foot down without trampling on the rights of others.*

9 *The best route to self-respect is first respecting others.*

10 *The assertive person's aim is to seek 'win/win' solutions where no one feels abused or used and everyone gets something of what they want or need.*

3

Knowing your rights

In this chapter you will learn:
- *that you have rights*
- *what you are entitled to*
- *how to consider priorities*
- *how to achieve your own 'Bill of Rights'.*

'I know my rights!' is most likely to be the cry of someone using aggression rather than assertion. But knowing or, more accurately, understanding and acknowledging your rights is actually an important part of being assertive. Whether you realize it or not, at the root of much non-assertive behaviour is a range of beliefs about your lack of rights. Before you can start gaining assertiveness skills and putting them into action you first need to consider what you should expect of yourself, and what others can expect of you.

What do you feel you're entitled to? Whether it's in our intimate relationships or with our family, with friends, with colleagues or in the world at large we all proceed with some assumptions about what we think is due to us. These assumptions set the way we relate with others, and feel about ourselves. Do any of these sound familiar? Are they things you might say?

'If someone asks me to do something I must have a good excuse before I can say no.'

'I must do things well or not do them at all.'

'My family should come before me.'

'I feel so stupid when I don't know something.'

'I don't like giving my opinions – what I say isn't important.'

'Oh no, I wouldn't try that – something may go wrong!'

'What other people think about me is really important to me.'

'When family members or friends or colleagues make a request, I ought to do as they ask.'

'People would think I'm rude or bossy if I stand up for my rights.'

'If people I know have problems I feel it's up to me to do something about them.'

'I'd rather give in than have a fight.'

If you answered yes to just one of those, this chapter is for you. Two or more and you *really* need to read on!

Your rights

You, just as much as any other person, have certain rights. This doesn't mean you should be in a dominant position over others, or that you should be able to make other people do what you want. What it does mean, however, is that you need to recognize that you have just as much claim as anyone else to what is due to you. You deserve just, morally good, legal, proper and fitting treatment, as does everyone around you. To become assertive you should first recognize that.

> ### Insight
> Knowing your rights isn't being a 'jobsworth' ('Oh, it's more than my job's worth to let you do that...'), nor is it being arrogant or unlikeable. It's being assertive and something that all of us should understand.

What rights does an assertive person lay claim to?

The right to say no. This is perhaps the most fundamental of all. We are, every day, surrounded by responsibilities, expectations and demands. Your partner may expect you collect the dry cleaning, your children may demand you drive them to friends, your family may assume you will visit, your friends that you will go out with them and your colleagues that you will finish that work they left. You may agree that some of these are down to you, some will be none of your business. But do you have the ability, do you feel you have the right, to say 'no' to any of them? Being assertive means knowing when you can, and that you should, say 'No, I'm not doing that.' The skill, of course, is in being able to do so while keeping yourself, and, where possible, other people, from feeling bad about it.

The right not to have to give excuses for our behaviour. Along with the right to say no, is the understanding that we don't have to explain ourselves when we do say it. If you go into a long and involved excuse, what you are actually saying is 'You have a right to know why I'm saying no.' Handing over that right to know also then implies 'You have a right to my time and attention' and following on from that 'Which means you have the right to come back and knock down my excuses and get what you want!' Which is what usually happens when we give excuses – the other person immediately tries to work around them. When you say no, you have your reasons; you don't have to explain them. Not doing so sends the powerful message 'I have assessed the situation and made my decision as is my right to do.'

The right to be listened to. We should expect other people to hear what we are saying. That's not the same as their having to fall in line with us or be swayed by us – that's their responsibility to decide. But everyone should have the right to expect other people to listen to what they say, to take it on board and value what is said as being an expression of their feelings and opinions.

The right to express personal opinions. You don't know everything – you may not know much – but you, as well as everyone else, has a right to say what you think and feel. Your opinions are your own and you have just as much right to own them, and to claim space to voice them, as anyone. Other people have the right to question your facts and debate the basis of your opinions and beliefs; what no one has the right to do is to stop you thinking or saying them or to deny that your opinions are yours, and have value for that reason.

The right to say 'I don't know'. We don't always have an answer or an opinion. Being assertive is knowing when to declare lack of knowledge and to know there's nothing wrong in doing so. It doesn't diminish you in any way to have areas where you lack knowledge or certainty, nor to say so.

The right to give and receive feedback. Feedback is when we respond to what someone has said or asked or done, or listen to what other people have to say about us and our behaviour. Giving and receiving feedback is an important part of communicating, negotiating and compromising, all vital skills in assertive behaviour. You need to feel free to offer feedback, and to ask for it, to be able to be assertive.

The right to make mistakes. Aggressive behaviour tends to rely on the belief that you don't, can't, make mistakes – any suggestion you have done so is the accuser's fault. Submissive behaviour goes with a conviction you make nothing but mistakes, and that making them is a great weakness. Assertive behaviour understands that we all make mistakes – it's normal and that's how we learn. Making mistakes is not a sign of moral weakness or stupidity – it's simply because we can't know everything and have to learn and practise skills. So one important aspect of assertiveness is knowing that mistakes are OK and neither to be avoided, glossed over or excused. You make a mistake, take the lesson and move on.

The right to change my mind. Politicians are particularly fond of refusing to back down, or denying it when they do make a U-turn as if a change of mind shows weakness or foolishness. In fact, changing your mind means you have weighed up new evidence and decided it should affect your position. It does not show an inability to know your own mind – on the contrary, it shows an ability to assess, consider and evaluate and it is an important right to claim.

The right to say 'that's not my responsibility'. We all have responsibilities – things that are ours to do and to be accountable for. But it's very easy to find yourself taking over other people's jobs – maybe because we feel to get them done well and on time it has to be down to us. It's equally easy to respond to other people's demands or requests to do things for them and take the burden off their shoulders. We often feel bad or selfish or mean if we don't accept other people's responsibilities as our own – to look out for them and after them. Being assertive is knowing when and how to say 'No – that's yours, not mine. You'll do it – I won't. And if you don't do it, it doesn't get done. That's not my business.'

The right to do things in my own way. Sometimes, what we do and how we do it can be done differently and maybe more efficiently. It's important to be able to say 'No, this is how I want to do this' and to be heard and left alone. You may, after reflection, change your mind – that's up to you. But what is essential is to be able to make that choice.

The right to be given respect. Whether other people agree with you or violently disagree, we should all respect each other's opinions and right to make our own decisions. Part of being assertive is to know that you have the right to be respected and accorded value.

The right to expect certain standards from other people. You cannot insist that other people do what you say or act as you want them to, just as you have the right to ask them not to expect you to fall in with their demands. But you do have the right to expect them to be respectful, responsible and honest, as you would like to be to them.

The right to be consulted when decisions might have an impact on me. Whether at home, with friends or at work, we should expect other people to take us and our wishes and needs into account when they make plans that affect us too.

The right to take appropriate risks. Sometimes we opt for the tried and tested, safe and easy route. But sometimes it's vital to step outside our comfort zone, take some risks and try something different, whether in our private or work lives. Just because you are a parent, a partner, somebody's child or somebody's employee or employer, doesn't mean you should always do what is expected and safe. We need to know we can take some risks sometimes, and be able to let other people know it's OK.

Insight

Saying 'No' may seem a negative choice but in fact it is often a very positive one. Saying 'No' to certain requests, suggestions, demands, expectations means that when you do say 'Yes' it has some force and weight – it is a considered choice and can thus be seen as a gift. If you always go along with what other people say you become a 'yes person', someone who slavishly agrees with everything. There's no satisfaction in getting a yes from them. But there is enormous satisfaction in getting a yes from someone who weighs up the options and only agrees when it is the right thing to do.

Essential points to consider

1 *Knowing your rights doesn't make you aggressive or obstructionist.*
2 *Your rights do not ride roughshod over anyone else's and neither do theirs over yours.*
3 *Saying 'No' is often a very positive choice.*

Case study

As a single mum with two children, Nikki found it particularly hard to recognize, let alone stand up for, her rights. She was insistent that her children had to come first at all times, which is admirable but meant she was run ragged looking after them and hardly sparing a thought for herself. Her two elder sisters assumed she would always be the one to pop round to see if their mum was alright because she lived nearer, even though one of them did not have children and the other was in a two-parent family. Nikki hated admitting she needed help, so seldom asked for it from her friends or her children's father. If she did back away from one more commitment, she always gave long and involved excuses, prompting whoever had asked to assume she'd do it some other time. We worked together and I suggested she start by thinking about just one right, and claiming it for her own. After some consideration she decided she needed to recognize she could say no. So she did it. When her sister rang and asked if she'd stop by their mum's that night on the way home from work, Nikki said 'No.' Her sister was obviously startled, 'Why not?' Nikki took a deep breath and simply said 'No. I can't.' To her amazement, her sister responded 'Oh, I'm so silly, I should have thought. I bet you have lots on. I'll go. I'll let you know how she is.' Nikki copied out the list of rights and said she was going to go through them, one by one.

Have a look at this table and tick what rights you feel you can claim at present:

RIGHTS	
To say 'no'	
To not give any reasons or excuses for my behaviour	
To be listened to	
To express personal opinions	
To say 'I don't know'	
To give and receive feedback	
To make a mistake	
To change my mind	
To say 'that's not my responsibility'	
To do things in my own way	
To be given respect	
To expect certain standards from other people	
To be consulted when decisions might have an impact on me	
To take appropriate risks	

Now have a look at this table and tick which rights you think your partner, family, friends and colleagues claim.

RIGHTS	Partner	Family	Friends	Colleagues
To say 'no'				
To not give any reasons or excuses for their behaviour				
To be listened to				
To express personal opinions				
To say 'I don't know'				
To give and receive feedback				
To make a mistake				
To change their mind				
To say 'that's not my responsibility'				
To do things in their own way				
To be given respect				
To expect certain standards from other people				
To be consulted when decisions might have an impact on them				
To take appropriate risks				

Insight

We often happily give away rights to other people that we hesitate to claim for ourselves. There's nothing selfish in treating yourself as well as you care for others.

Do other people seem to have a lot more ticks than you have given yourself? What are the main rights and responsibilities that you now see should be observed by both parties in all your relationships?

RIGHTS	Me	Partner	Family	Friends	Colleagues
To say 'no'					
To not give any reasons or excuses for my their behaviour					

RIGHTS	Me	Partner	Family	Friends	Colleagues
To be listened to					
To express personal opinions					
To say 'I don't know'					
To give and receive feedback					
To make a mistake					
To change my/their mind					
To say 'that's not my responsibility'					
To do things in my/their own way					
To be given respect					
To expect certain standards from other people					
To be consulted when decisions might have an impact on me/them					
To take appropriate risks					

Upholding your rights

How does upholding your own rights work in reality? It's all very well to read about these and think about them in theory, but what do you do when you come up against other people in the big, wide world?

Being assertive is showing appropriate self-interest. You're a member of many communities. You're a member of society, of a family, perhaps of a couple, maybe of a workplace and a friendship group. In all of those groups there are times when it's correct that you think of others and act accordingly. Perhaps you're the one who stands for ages holding open the shop door while people get in out of the rain. Or you drive someone in the family to an event when you'd rather be at home curled up in front of the TV.

Or you go to a film you know your partner will love... and you won't. Or you give up your day off to help at work when there is a rush on, or meet friends for a drink even though you'll have to catch up the time for something else you had to do. All of those can be a constructive part of your life. But being assertive is knowing when it's time to say 'I have to think of myself here.' Sometimes we need to say no or ask for a different arrangement to suit our needs too.

Insight

If you want to look after other people – partners, family, friends or work colleagues – first you have to look after yourself. You're no good to them if you're exhausted, resentful and confused because you haven't been able to stick up for yourself. If for no other reason than for other people, it's important to know your rights and stand by them.

Being assertive is maintaining integrity. Fitting in with other people, fostering their self-esteem and supporting them are important parts of getting by. But sometimes not only do we have to say no, we need to foster our own self-esteem and support ourselves. That means that there are times when you should, and should feel able to, take a stand or voice your own dissenting opinions, if you are to feel good about yourself.

Insight

Assertiveness can involve defending your rights, while respecting others' rights.

Assertiveness can involve carrying out your responsibilities while insisting others also adhere to their responsibilities.

Considering your priorities

One of the key points in asserting yourself and claiming your rights is to consider your priorities. You undermine yourself and don't send clear messages about where you wish to stand and how others should respond to you if you have these confused. You need to think about what you feel is non-negotiable, what you might compromise and what is actually unimportant. You stand a much better chance of getting what you need and want if your requests are appropriate. Using all your weight on a matter that is actually unimportant means when it comes to what should be a non-negotiable issue you can't make the distinction. For instance, making it a matter of life and death when a teenager wants to go out wearing clothes you feel are a mess might mean you have trouble insisting they don't get into a car driven by a friend who has been drinking.

Chew over these scenarios and tick which category you feel they come under, at the moment:

	Non-negotiable	Compromise	Unimportant
It's my birthday and my partner is taking me out. At the last moment, a family member says I have to give them a lift to see a friend.			
A friend asks me to join them on a weekend away and when I say no, demands to know why.			
A family member often leaves coffee cups in their room.			
When I express an opinion, someone close to me keeps saying 'You don't mean that!'			
Now I know the full story, I've changed my mind over something but I've been told 'You can't do that!'			
I catch a bus that is often empty but a particular person always jumps the queue.			

(Contd)

	Non-negotiable	Compromise	Unimportant
Holiday leave has been decided, and nobody asked me when I wanted to go.			
If I say 'I don't know' someone I know says 'You ought to – you're stupid!'			
I want to do something totally new this weekend – my friends and family are more cautious.			

Take a moment to consider your answers. Are there times or situations where you might feel differently about your priorities?

Consider who you need to please and impress

Most of the problems we fall into come about because we try so hard to please other people – our family, our friends, our employers. It dates back to wanting to please and be appreciated by our parents. One good tip for passing on assertiveness to your children is to help them cultivate the habit of looking to themselves for approval before they look elsewhere. If you only think well of yourself when your worth is reflected through other people's eyes, you are forever at the mercy of their interests. Of course, some of the people you encounter will want the best for you and be sympathetic, kind and enabling. But some will give you approval only as it suits them – when what you are doing pleases them rather than benefits you. Think of the parents who only say their child is being good and acceptable when that child is doing what they want, rather than what might be right for the child. Think of the partners who only say they love you if you're doing what they say. Or the friends who only applaud you if you're falling in with their plans. What we need is children who can answer the question 'Are you pleased with what you have done? Are you satisfied and full of self-worth?' with a YES! And you need to be able to do that for yourself, too. If you didn't have the good fortune to be helped to be proud of yourself when young you can do it now.

....

Insight

Every day, ask yourself 'What did I do today that I can be pleased about and proud of? What can I do tomorrow that will content me?' Praise yourself and then you can enjoy plaudits from others, but not be dependent on their approval.

....

This is a poem written by Dale Wimbrow, published in 1934. In spite of being of the time, and therefore only talking to men, it still has a vital message to anyone considering being assertive. ('Pelf', by the way, means money.)

The Guy in the Glass

When you get what you want in your struggle for pelf,
And the world makes you King for a day,
Then go to the mirror and look at yourself,
And see what that guy has to say.

For it isn't your Father or Mother or Wife,
Who judgement upon you must pass.
The feller whose verdict counts most in your life
Is the guy staring back from the glass.

He's the feller to please, never mind all the rest,
For he's with you clear up to the end,
And you've passed your most dangerous, difficult test
If the guy in the glass is your friend.

You may be like Jack Horner and 'chisel' a plum,
And think you're a wonderful guy,
But the man in the glass says you're only a bum
If you can't look him straight in the eye.

You can fool the whole world down the pathway of years,
And get pats on the back as you pass,
But your final reward will be heartaches and tears
If you've cheated the guy in the glass.

10 THINGS TO REMEMBER

1 *Recognizing you have rights is the foundation of assertiveness skills.*

2 *If you never say 'No', it diminishes the worth of your 'Yes'.*

3 *You have equal importance to other people – not more but not less.*

4 *Having your rights considered doesn't mean ignoring or overriding those of other people.*

5 *You don't have to give excuses or even explanations when you say no.*

6 *You are responsible for yourself. Sometimes and in some circumstances you can assume responsibility for others, but you have the right to explore and examine these.*

7 *Just because someone wants to dump responsibility on you doesn't mean you have to accept it.*

8 *You can't make other people take on their responsibilities or stand up for themselves. But by caring for yourself and asserting your rights and responsibilities, you can model how it is done while protecting yourself.*

9 *Allowing other people to ride roughshod over you will not make them or even allow them to do the right thing. Standing up for yourself, however, gives them the opportunity to make that choice too.*

10 *Consider your priorities. Some issues are vital and non-negotiable. Others may be negotiable and some, on reflection, may be unimportant. Sometimes we muddy the water by getting sidetracked into deadlocked arguments over issues that really don't matter, and then cannot assert ourselves over truly important issues.*

EXERCISE

How might all this translate in your personal and working life?
This might be the basic 'Bill of Rights' that all of us should expect
and accept:

1 *I have the right to say 'no'.*

2 *I have the right to not give any reasons or excuses for
   my behaviour.*

3 *I have the right to be listened to.*

4 *I have the right to express personal opinions.*

5 *I have the right to say 'I don't know'.*

6 *I have the right to give and receive feedback.*

7 *I have the right to make a mistake.*

8 *I have the right to change my mind.*

9 *I have the right to say 'that's not my responsibility'.*

10 *I have the right to do things in my own way.*

11 *I have the right to be given respect.*

12 *I have the right to expect certain standards from other people.*

13 *I have the right to be consulted when decisions might have an
    impact on me.*

14 *I have the right to take appropriate risks.*

But you might like to draw up your own list of things that are
important to you and that you might like to insist are accorded

respect and kept to, by yourself and those around you. Here are some suggestions based on my own high priority issues. You can add and subtract according to yours!

My personal Bill of Rights:

1 *I have the right to let you know about my day and have you listen.*

2 *I have the right to have you tell me about your day.*

3 *I have the right to have a night without TV, talking.*

4 *I have the right for us to share household chores equally.*

5 *I have the right for us to share family tasks equally.*

6 *I have the right to exercise three times a week – at least!*

7 *I have the right to time on my own.*

8 *I have the right to time with you.*

9 *I have the right to time for us all as a family.*

10 *I have the right to have any requests I make listened to and treated with respect.*

11 *I have the right to be silly sometimes.*

12 *I have the right to be 'off duty' and not to be in charge.*

13 *I have the right to make suggestions and have them considered.*

Make your own list. It doesn't only have to be rights you feel comfortable claiming at present but also rights you might like to lay claim to as we go on. Keep the list nearby and see how those issues important to you become more attainable as we go on in later chapters.

4

....

Responsibilities

In this chapter you will learn:
- *the responsibilities that go with rights*
- *the fears and anxieties of change*
- *about taking risks*
- *about 'SWOT' charts – Strengths, Weaknesses, Opportunities and Threats.*

Responsibilities and the fear of change

We've looked at the rights you can lay claim to, and considered the importance of recognizing you have them. On the surface, anyone might think that's enough to make becoming assertive very appealing. After all, who can resist being given such advantages, and who can believe not having or exercising your rights is an attractive proposition?

But there are some downsides to standing up for yourself. We need to explore them because it's the recognition or realization that there are other sides to this that hold you back, even if you haven't realized that is what is happening.

With rights go responsibilities

With rights go responsibilities – and it's these that can make taking action and becoming assertive difficult. If you become assertive and claim your rights, you can no longer hide behind excuses. 'I was late because I couldn't get away' is not something an assertive person says. Nor can you blame other people – 'It's all your fault' can no longer be in your vocabulary. Becoming assertive might make you feel uncomfortable because you have to stick your head above the parapet – you have to take decisions and stand by them. There are pay-offs to taking on responsibilities and making changes. Pay-offs, however, can be felt to be both negative and positive. We'll need to confront our own fears and anxieties about becoming assertive before we can go any further.

Change is always hard

Insight

The truth is that change is always hard, always scary and always difficult. And that's true whether the changes we foresee are to our advantage or we expect them to be to our disadvantage. It's the process of change that is uncomfortable, whatever the end result.

We live in a society that is changing at a rate probably never seen before. When I was growing up parents and children were forever at loggerheads because we'd get home from school and then hog the family phone talking to our friends. Now, it's mobile phones and the internet, and a type and expectation of almost full-time connectivity that our grandparents would have believed was the stuff of science fiction. I could name some social networking sites that most of us over 25 never even dreamed of when we were kids – but by the time you read this they may well have been superseded by the next new thing!

What initiatives such as these have meant is that most of us have had to get used to things rapidly evolving and becoming different. Change has always been something we struggle with, whether a change for the better or the worse. The stress around making adjustments to our lives seems more acute now since it is so common. But it's how we view change and either embrace it, try to avoid it or become downright terrified of it, that can affect how you manage. We have to make more and more effort to keep up, yet we are constantly bombarded with messages that tell us the new and the desirable is labour-saving, easy and simple. It's a contradiction that can make people stressed. Far from being exciting and helpful, we can find making any alteration in our lives and our behaviour is difficult and stressful.

Taking risks

We are a 'risk-averse' culture. Most of us feel meddling may make things more, not less, difficult, so it's far better to stay with a known quantity and keep things as they are. We don't like taking risks, in case it is for the worse, and this often works against us seeking change. We may hold back from acting and becoming more assertive because:

- ▶ *I could make a fool of myself, trying to assert myself and failing.*
- ▶ *I could upset other people by trying to get above myself.*
- ▶ *If I tried to change and didn't manage it, I might make my life more difficult than it already is.*
- ▶ *You shouldn't meddle, because you'll make it worse.*
- ▶ *If it ain't broke don't fix it.*

The problem is that if you're reading this, it is broke and it does need fixing! Take the risk – what is the worst that can happen? You might fear you'd fail and feel awful or that people would laugh at you or take even more advantage of you because you tried and were unsuccessful. In fact, the worst that can happen is that you're just the same as you were. So why not try, because if it can't get worse, it may get a whole lot better?

What could happen if you try to change?

What we imagine is going to happen if we make changes is far worse than the reality. How many times have you geared yourself up to doing something, avoiding it or dreading it, and then afterwards say 'Oh, that wasn't so bad after all!' Our fears are frequently out of proportion to the actual situation, and we simply don't factor in the benefits that will come from going ahead. The worst case scenario of trying is often this:

▶ *You tried and didn't manage it… this time. It takes time and effort to change yourself, your beliefs and your behaviour. You can always try again, a bit at a time, slowly over a period. One setback is only that – a setback, not a failure.*
▶ *You tried and didn't manage it… but learned something. Each time you make an attempt you gain valuable hints as to what went wrong and what you could do next time to make it work.*
▶ *You tried and didn't manage it… but gave everyone else something to think about. When you step outside the box you alert those around you to the fact that you aren't prepared to go on as you have done up to then. They may not take you so much for granted any more, especially when you try again.*

That's the worst case scenario. The actual reality is likely to be this:

▶ *You tried and were pleasantly surprised at how much easier it was than you thought.*
▶ *You tried and realized a few small changes could add up to big differences.*
▶ *You tried and found those around you were encouraging.*
▶ *You tried and found although it took effort, the results were worth it.*

BEING SCARED ISN'T SO BAD

Being scared of change and of taking on responsibility for yourself is a natural anxiety. One way of dealing with it is to recognize that being scared isn't that awful an emotion to experience. Indeed, sometimes we deliberately court it and enjoy it – what are horror films and roller-coasters about other than being ways of making us frightened for fun? We seek out frights sometimes because the reaction we have to fear – an adrenaline rush, pounding heart, sweaty palms – is exhilarating. Overcoming fear and working with it and through it is an essential part of personal development. If you avoid something that frightens you, the fear does not go away – in fact, it can grow. If you face it, you can begin to confront it and conquer it. By facing a fear, you can remove its power to intimidate you and so build up your self-confidence and self-esteem.

Insight

Being overwhelmed by anxieties and doubts are what holds us back from becoming assertive. We think we hold back from trying because we will fail and be laughed at or have the situation made worse. But the **fear** of being made weak and powerless, when in fact we may be able to triumph if we tried, is what actually hampers us.

The other person is not making you do anything: you are

This is the big secret of being assertive:

Nobody can do to you what you refuse to have done.

Another person cannot make you do anything, unless you agree to do it. Another person cannot take away your power, unless you give it to them.

When you are late for a meeting because someone else makes you stay, or babysit for a friend when you have other things you want to do, or go out when you'd rather stay in that night, unless you've been kidnapped, tied up, had your car keys confiscated or the door locked on you, the other person is not making you do anything: you are.

But of course, in the back of your mind, you may already know this. And that's one of the first and vital choices about becoming assertive. Because being a victim, being someone whom other people push around and tell what to do, can actually be quite a comfortable, safe position. By handing over responsibility for yourself you may feel secure and blame-free – someone else has to shoulder the work and the culpability. There are upsides to being looked after. In considering becoming more assertive you need to recognize, acknowledge and accept why you may have chosen to be non-assertive, and what you will need to both lose and gain in making new choices.

Case study

Steve had worked as a postman in a small town for over 15 years. He was due to retire in two years and was dreading it. He was fit, active and had no desire to garden or redecorate his home, as all the friends who had retired before him seemed to be doing. Then he was offered a business opportunity, to become a courier for local firms. The upside was that it would be better paid and more interesting, flexible work. The downside was that being freelance it could be a risk. Some of Steve's family and friends, including his wife and two sons, were pessimistic. What if the situation changed? He wouldn't have the security of his post office job. What if the work proved too tiring? He wasn't getting any younger. Steve was about to turn down the offer when his wife talked it through with some friends. She had been cautious and frightened of taking the risk until she had a chance to think about all the pros and cons. She went home and pointed out that the security would only last two years anyway, and he was certainly up for it for that period. He would enjoy the challenge, and if it got too much after his retirement date he could always pass it on with no loss. Steve took the job and five years later is still going strong, with one employee and a far bigger bank balance.

A few years ago I took my two godsons for an afternoon on a giant aerial obstacle course using ladders, zip wires, walkways, bridges and tunnels made of wood, rope and wire. The course ended with the 'Tarzan Leap' – you jumped from a platform, swung out over a precipice on a rope and had to let go to land in a net. You were, of course, totally secure in harnesses and safety lines, but it was scary to say the least. Ahead of us was a young girl who stood and then sat hesitating on the edge for a full 20 minutes. She was scared but she didn't want to go back – she just couldn't go forward. Eventually she launched and I shall always remember her scream of pure joy and delight, not just at the rush from the jump but the elation of having taken the risk, by choice.

1 *With rights go responsibilities. It is this that can make learning to be assertive complicated.*
2 *Change, even good change, is always hard, scary and difficult.*
3 *We live in a risk-averse society and tend to think 'If it ain't broke don't fix it.'*
4 *Another person cannot make you do anything unless you agree and cannot take power away from you unless you give it.*

Insight

Becoming assertive requires you to take responsibility for yourself and to make choices. But it's important to recognize that *not* being assertive, perhaps staying as you are, is equally a choice. When we decide *not* to do something, that is as active a decision as to make up your mind to act. Both require energy. Which is why I suggest that if you're going to expend thought and effort on doing something, choose the path that leads to the resolution with a better outcome for yourself and perhaps for others too.

Strengths, Weaknesses, Opportunities and Threats

Once we've recognized our rights and looked at how we might take responsibility and make choices, the obvious question is 'How can we do this?' The first step is to SWOT.

SWOT stands for Strengths, Weaknesses, Opportunities and Threats.

Your **Strengths** are what you do well. We all have strengths, even if we don't realize what they might be. The trick is to recognize them, accept and develop them and use them, to our best advantage.

Your **Weaknesses** are what you do less well. We all have them too, even the people we look up to and think are better than us. The trick is to recognize and accept them as well, and to see how we can work around them so they don't pull us down.

Your **Opportunities**. You may not realize this but all around you may be things – other people, ideas, situations – that you can benefit from to achieve what you want and need.

Your **Threats**. While your weaknesses are the issues inside you that might hold you back, threats are the things outside that could sabotage you.

	These help you get what you want	These stop you getting what you want
Inside you Outside you	STRENGTHS OPPORTUNITIES	WEAKNESSES THREATS

Becoming assertive means looking at the things that can help you, both inside and out – your strengths and opportunities – and increasing each. It means looking at the things that can hinder you, both inside and out – your weaknesses and threats – and diminishing each.

This exercise can help you work out what you might need to do. In the chart, I've filled in some of my strengths and opportunities, weaknesses and threats, with a particular goal in mind: to lose some weight.

	These help you get what you want	These stop you getting what you want
Inside you	STRENGTHS A positive outlook. I like exercise. I can work hard.	WEAKNESSES I love chocolate! I can be tempted to eat fattening foods. I can be put off going to the gym.

	These help you get what you want	These stop you getting what you want
Inside you	I know what I need to do. I prefer food cooked from scratch.	
Outside you	OPPORTUNITIES My husband wants to lose weight as well. It's spring so the garden needs work. Fresh fruit and salad are in the shops.	THREATS Demands on my time mean I can miss gym appointments. Bad weather can make it difficult to go out walking or gardening

How can we use and get the most out of each Strength? In this case, I can benefit from having a generally positive outlook to bolster me up when my enthusiasm is flagging. I can use the fact that I know I get a kick out of exercise to tell myself I'll feel better when I've been to the gym – experience tells me I'm right so each time I go I can make a mental note to remember how I feel the next time I'm hesitating. The fact that I can work hard means when I do go, I don't waste my visit – I put plenty of effort into it. I know how much fitness work I should be doing and what foods I should be eating and avoiding, and since I prefer home-cooked food I avoid all the sugars and fats in convenience food.

How can we improve each Weakness? I know that if I have chocolate and other fattening food around I will eat it. And that if it's cold or wet I can tell myself 'You don't need to go out to exercise today!' So I use some of my strengths to make sure I don't buy those temptations, and to cheer myself on when I want to avoid doing the right thing.

How can we exploit and benefit from each Opportunity? Looking around I can see that the fact that my husband would also like to lose some weight is a great help – we can encourage each other to do exercise, in the gym and garden, and to enjoy healthy meals together. I can harness his enthusiasm to increase mine.

How can we lessen each Threat? When I'm busy it's very easy to run out of time and not have enough to do the things I know are good for me – to exercise and to prepare fresh meals. Knowing this in advance means I can make special efforts to arrange my diary so I fit everything in.

Essential points to consider

1   *If you are going to expend time and effort on something, choose the path that should have the best outcome for you.*
2   *Doing the SWOT test and finding your Strengths, Weaknesses, Opportunities and Threats should set you on a true course towards assertiveness.*
3   *You can always find a way of putting some sort of positive spin on the most negative of situations.*

Now fill in your SWOT chart. Thinking about being assertive – what are your strengths and opportunities, weaknesses and threats?

	These help you get what you want	*These stop you getting what you want*
Inside you	STRENGTHS	WEAKNESSES

	These help you get what you want	These stop you getting what you want
Outside you	OPPORTUNITIES	THREATS

Insight

We can make threats into opportunities, weaknesses into strengths not just by using our opposite strengths or opportunities to balance them; we can also do so by looking at them differently and twisting them to our advantage. Sometimes, it's our attitude that makes the difference.

MAKING A THREAT INTO AN OPPORTUNITY

You can and have to put a positive spin on the most negative trait or situation. How's this for one way to take a rejection?

Thank you for your letter of March 16. After careful consideration, I regret to inform you that I am unable to accept your refusal to offer me an assistant professor position in your department.

This year I have been particularly fortunate in receiving an unusually large number of rejection letters. With such a varied and promising field of candidates, it is impossible for me to accept all refusals.

Despite your outstanding qualifications and previous experience in rejecting applicants, I find that your rejection does not meet my needs at this time. Therefore, I will assume the position of assistant professor in your department this August. I look forward to seeing you then.

Best of luck in rejecting future applicants.

Sincerely,

10 THINGS TO REMEMBER

1 *With rights go responsibilities.*

2 *The process of change is always uncomfortable.*

3 *We live in a risk-averse society which encourages us to hold back from taking action.*

4 *'If it ain't broke, don't fix it' is a good motto, unless it is broke and does need fixing!*

5 *Don't let fear of failure hold you back. The worst that can happen is you stay the same.*

6 *Have a go – things just might get a whole lot better.*

7 *Overcoming fear, and working with and through it, is an essential part of our development.*

8 *For inspiration and encouragement, think about that girl on the platform. Don't be afraid to jump off!.*

9 *Use the SWOT chart technique to start you off. Reuse it as you progress to keep up your resolve.*

10 *Nobody can make you do anything. It is you who gives away your power and does it for them. Say no and keep control of your own choices.*

EXERCISE

Be like the assistant professor. Think about where you are in your life at the moment. What rejection or piece of bad luck or lost opportunity would you like to turn around? Sit down and write you own 'rejection of a rejection' letter.

Then consider how you might put that rejection of rejection into action. Write down what skills you might need, what changes in your abilities you might want. Read on and find tricks and strategies for doing so.

Beliefs and values

In this chapter you will learn:
- *about examining your beliefs and values*
- *how to change obstructive thoughts into helpful ones*
- *how to deal with your strengths and weaknesses*
- *about the power of language – and how to change yours*
- *how to deal with generalizations and self-fulfilling prophecies.*

Your beliefs can hold you back

In the journey to becoming assertive you may well find your beliefs about yourself can hold you back. One of the important steps to being able to stand up for yourself is to examine what beliefs and values you hold, how they may be affecting you and what you can do to change them.

What sort of beliefs hamper and hinder you? Look at the following and see if any of them sound familiar:

▶ *I'm no good at anything.*
▶ *Everyone else always seems to know what they're doing.*
▶ *I don't deserve it.*
▶ *People don't change.*
▶ *My needs aren't as important as other people's.*
▶ *My partner and kids should always come first.*

Insight

Most of us can hear a voice telling us 'You're no good', 'You shouldn't get above yourself', 'People can't change so why bother'. The strange thing is that if someone said these things to you, out loud and to your face, you'd probably react by saying 'How dare you! What right do you have to say that?' But since it's you talking, or a memory of people you love and trust such as a parent, you put up with it and believe it. Until now, that is. This is where and when you start talking back!

Changing the voice

Negative beliefs such as these undermine us. Before you can even begin to practise assertive behaviour you need to change the voice you hear telling you what you are, and are not, capable of to a positive one. If you don't value yourself, it's hard for other people to value you. If other people don't value you, that may be their problem, not yours, or because your beliefs about yourself are getting in the way of them from doing so.

It becomes far easier to act assertively once we have a sense of our own self-worth. Self-esteem and self-confidence are tightly bound up with an ability to know what we should expect to be due to us. You can act assertively if what you believe about yourself is that:

▶ *I have many skills and abilities.*
▶ *I am deserving.*
▶ *I can change my behaviour and so can you.*
▶ *My needs are as important as, but not more or less than, other people's.*

In contrast, acting unassertively proceeds from a low sense of self-worth and from low self-esteem and confidence. But there is one important thing to remember when you are feeling put upon and hard done by. Eleanor Roosevelt once said 'No one can make you feel inferior without your consent.' And she was right.

Beliefs are powerful and important

There is no doubt that the beliefs that other people instil in you are powerful and important. If you've been brought up being told, at worst, you're useless or, at best, 'Don't worry, dear, you can't expect to go far...' it can be difficult to fight against those beliefs. Other people's lack of faith in you rapidly translates to an absence of conviction in yourself. You may not even remember it started with other people; by now, it's ingrained and part of you. Every time you try and fail you confirm in yourself your lack of ability. What you miss is that your failures may occur because you don't have any confidence, or that they aren't actually failures at all but you only see the negative, not the positive. What you miss, most of all, is that you give away your strength. You collude and conspire to make yourself substandard.

Case study

Jez and Zarqa came to me for couple counselling with problems in their relationship. One important aspect that emerged was that Zarqa felt their relationship was doomed – her mother always told her she'd not amount to much, and what man worth his salt would put up with her? Jez adored her, but she simply didn't believe he could love a waste of space like her. We explored her beliefs and whether they stood up to examination, and whether she should go on clinging to them simply because of how long she had had them, and where they originated. By 'examining the voice' Zarqa began to see how her mother's own lack of self-esteem and confidence had resulted in her being critical and judgemental. When she could forgive her mother for this she could also begin to banish the voice, and recognize her own value.

To take this important step towards assertiveness, you need to learn to talk to yourself in the way you would like someone else who wants to be supportive and effective to talk to you – a good friend, a professional counsellor, a loving and caring parent. What you need is for that voice to aid you in banishing obstructive thoughts and replacing them with helpful ones: to be affirming, encouraging, challenging and supportive.

Practising affirmative thoughts

Each day, when you are getting ready in the bathroom – washing your face, cleaning your teeth, either putting on make-up or shaving – take a few minutes to look at yourself and tell yourself a few new home truths. Go through the following, and choose what best fits your needs, depending on what the nasty voice is telling you at present:

I'm no good at anything. Oh yes you are! Everyone has at least one thing they do really well. And most of us have a whole range of things, if we only recognized it or were prepared to brush aside the nay-saying and get on with it. Go on – ask yourself what do you do well, and see what pops into your mind. It can be something silly and apparently trivial or something really important. Once you begin to look, you'll find there is a range of things you do that you can be justifiably proud of. What should you be telling yourself? *I am good at many things – I should be proud of my skills, and on the look out for more to add to the list.*

Everyone else always seems to know what they're doing. They may seem to but that doesn't mean they do. We all bluff and cover up and when you're convinced you're all at sea and everyone else has it sussed, the likelihood is that everyone else is just as uncertain about themselves, and just as convinced *you* know what you're doing. What should you be telling yourself? *I'm the same as everyone else – sometimes we know what we're doing and sometimes we don't. So what?*

I don't deserve it. When you want something, or when good things happen, this unkind voice may tell you that you haven't earned it or aren't worthy of it. But you have and you are – trust me! You work hard, you look after other people and you make sure they get what they merit. It's time to extend that generosity to yourself. What should you be telling yourself? *I deserve good things – I've earned them!*

People don't change. It's easy to feel you're stuck as who you are, and that other people will always be the way they are. None of that is true. You can't change other people but you can certainly choose to act differently, feel differently and be a different person – and so can others. What should you be telling yourself? *I'm not stuck – I can change if I want to.*

My needs aren't as important as other people's. So what makes them so special and you so ordinary? Someone may have said so sometime in your life and others may have never contradicted this so you've accepted it. But it simply isn't true. Your needs have equal weight with everyone else's and you have just as much right to be considered – and that's a fact. What should you be telling yourself? *My needs are as important as anyone else's.*

My partner and kids should always come first. Often we have to put children first – they're dependent on us, we chose to have them and we're the grown-ups so we have the capability to put our own needs on hold until theirs are satisfied. And there are times when we may choose to care for our partner and cater for them before ourselves. But sometimes we should be first in the queue. Children need to learn how to wait their turn and that parents have needs too – that's an important and healthy lesson for them to learn. And putting a partner first should be a reciprocal or give-and-take exchange – they care for you as often as you care for them. If you don't look after yourself you may not have the energy to look after them when they need you, so if for no other reason, sometimes you need to put yourself first. What should you be telling yourself? *Sometimes, I should come first.*

WHAT SHOULD YOUR MESSAGES BE?

Some of these messages may help you, some may not and you may realize your own particular issues are not covered. To explore what beliefs may be hampering you, a good strategy is to sit down and write out your beliefs. Get a big sheet of paper, or set up a table on your computer, and have two columns headed 'Good' and 'Bad'. Under 'Good', list as many positive statements as you can think of about yourself. It often helps to begin each with 'I am…', 'I can…', 'I do…', 'I will…'. Then, under 'Bad' list all the negative statements; 'I am not…', 'I cannot…', 'I don't…', 'I will not…'.

Insight

Make sure that for every negative you do a positive – and look for an upside to every negative. For instance, I would list that I'm terrible at languages – I was never good at them in school and now I have such difficulty swotting up on French or Spanish for when I go on holiday. The upside is that I try extra hard when dealing with people when I am abroad. If I can't remember the words, I make myself as pleasant as possible to get by instead – I smile, I use sign language and I make sure I know how to say the essentials of 'please', 'sorry' and 'thank you'. Knowing my limitations but not seeing it as a failure, I don't get into a panic about making a fool of myself – I look forward to doing what I can, and doing it well.

Consider your lists and rank your statement in order of importance. It's much more important, for instance, that 'I talk often with and can communicate well with my family', than 'I can't speak French'.

MAXIMIZE THE UPS AND MINIMIZE THE DOWNS

When you have your list, consider it. Focus first on what, where and when you do well, and then on what, where and when you do not. How can you maximize the ups and minimize the downs? Look at and concentrate on what you can do rather than what you can't. You might be disappointed that after watching all the food programmes on TV, you're still not a gourmet chef. Under 'Good' however, you might list that you make eating the evening meal a time and place for your family to come together and share. That's far more important than the actual food you serve. You might, for instance, want to rearrange schedules and commitments to increase the number of times in the week the family get together round a table to eat and chat.

Take your list to friends and family and ask for feedback on your strengths and weaknesses. What do they feel about what you have listed and the importance you attach to each part? Together, can you come up with more ideas to play down the problematical parts and give more space to the things you feel you do well?

1 *Examine the beliefs you hold, how they might affect you and how you might change some of them.*
2 *Talk to yourself the way you'd talk to someone you wanted to support.*
3 *For every negative thought add a positive one – and look for the upsides of the negatives too.*
4 *Ask friends and family you trust for feedback.*

The language you use is important

Your aim will be to change unhelpful thoughts – 'I can't do this', 'I'm bad at that' – into helpful ones – 'I have a talent for this', 'I excel at that'. Looking at the power of the language you often use can be instructive.

When we're not feeling positive about ourselves, the language we use reflects this. What we say, particularly to describe ourselves and our abilities, is overwhelmingly negative. How often do you find yourself saying:

▶ *can't*
▶ *don't*
▶ *won't*
▶ *mustn't*
▶ *oughtn't.*

Or even using lukewarm statements when people ask you if you'd like to do something or to describe your abilities:

▶ *okay*
▶ *all right*

- ▶ *go on then*
- ▶ *I suppose so.*

And even when you do say 'Yes' or 'I'll do that' or 'I can…', find yourself qualifying it with 'but…', 'however', 'except…'. 'I'll help you make tea but I'm awful at making scones', 'I can write that report for you however I won't be able to manage the maths', 'I'll arrange the meeting except I can't speak myself'. If you need some help or have something extra to say, a better word to use, which is positive, is 'and': '….and I'll need some support at making the scones/doing the maths/making the speech'. Use 'and', and all of a sudden, you can do it. You're not promising anything you can't handle, you are asking for a supportive hand, but most important of all, you're telling them and yourself you can do it.

Insight

There is no shame in asking for help or saying you need some support. We tend to try to bluff or avoid admitting either mistakes or a lack of skill when we should be seeing it as an opportunity to learn something.

Try this as an exercise. For the rest of the day, watch your words very carefully. Every time you use, or are about to use, a negative, take a deep breath and replace it – if necessary, by reframing what you said – with a positive statement.

For example:

	You might have said:	*Instead try:*
Do you want a coffee?	No, I don't.	I'd love a tea.
Let's see that film tonight.	Ugh, no, I hate that actor.	I'd love to go out, let's see the other one.
Want sauce on that?	No, I don't.	It's fine, thank you.

(Contd)

	You might have said:	*Instead try:*
Can you swim?	I'm all right I suppose.	Yes, I can.
Like some cake?	Oh go on then.	Yes, I'd love some thank you.
Can you do this?	No, I can't.	Yes I can and I'd like some support so I get it right.
Mum, can you drive me to town?	No, I'm too busy.	I can if you give me half an hour. And I'd be ready sooner if you did the washing up.
Join us on Friday?	I suppose so.	That would be lovely.
Have a chocolate?	I mustn't.	I'm eating healthily today.
Stay a bit later.	I oughtn't.	I'm up early tomorrow so I'll be off.

CHANGING THE WORDS CHANGES MORE THAN THE MEANING

Purposefully changing your language may seem artificial, ineffective or trivializing the situation, but it can have powerful effects. When some companies brought over the American habit of saying 'Have a nice day' to everyone it may have seem forced and unnatural but most people now recognize it does work. Having it said may be a matter of company policy, but it does alter the atmosphere for the better.

Insight
The language you use defines you, in your own eyes and in the eyes of those around you, and defines the situations you find yourself in.

IT LIMITS YOU

Statements such as 'I can't', 'I ought', 'I never', 'I don't deserve', 'No one likes me' limit your belief in yourself and your ability to change and develop. As we've already discussed, that can seem like an advantage – it means you can avoid taking on responsibility. But the risks are what make you unhappy and uncomfortable because negative language can result in your getting stuck in unhelpful patterns.

Take a sheet of paper, or set up a table on your computer, and fill in as many statements as you can that sound familiar to you:

I can't	
I don't	
I won't	
I mustn't	
I must	
I oughtn't	
I ought	
I shouldn't	
I should	
I don't deserve	
I never	
I always	

Then ask yourself these questions:

How do you know that? When you say 'can't,' what evidence do you have? If you've not been able to do something in the past, that's no reason to conclude you'll never be able to manage it. A bit of confidence, a bit of practice or a bit of support would all have you learning a skill or displaying a talent that you might not have realized or recognized you had or were perfectly capable of developing. You don't know you *can't* until you've tried without that voice in your head saying 'You're not going to be able to do this.' Replace it with a voice that says 'It may take time and preparation but I can do this' and see what happens.

Can I be specific? We often send out unclear messages when we feel unassertive. We don't just say 'I can't do this' when referring to a particular issue but descend into a general grumble of 'It's all so hard...', 'No one ever listens to me...', 'What can you do?' When this happens you need to ask yourself 'How?', 'In what way?', 'How do you know?' Requiring yourself to be specific means you often discover the problem is less than you thought, because you can't come up with many – or any – specific examples. You're expecting to be thwarted, and talking yourself into feeling ineffective and incapable.

What stops you? When you say 'don't, won't, mustn't, shouldn't, oughtn't', is it fear that prevents you trying – fear of failure, of humiliation, of being laughed at? Or of having to step up and be judged? Or is it memories, past or present, of someone saying 'You shouldn't do this' or 'We don't do that'? Is it fair? Is it just? Is it someone else's problem you're being landed with here? Maybe someone you know or knew thought these things – why should you? Examine what stops you, carefully and clearly; you may want to push the barrier aside.

What makes you? When you say 'must, ought, should' is it anxiety that pushes you on – are you scared of being scolded or disappointing someone if you don't do this? And, again, is it a realistic, present anxiety or one from your past, still affecting you? There is a difference between things that are truly necessary in our own lives, and those that we continue feeling are our responsibility or have to be done which are hangovers from past guilt or another person's belief. You don't 'have' to do anything – you choose to do them, and sometimes you need to revisit that choice and make new ones.

Who told you that? When you say 'don't deserve, never, always', whose voice do you hear? In most of the negative language or strictures we employ, if we think about it we can hear the voice that originally instilled this belief in us. A family member? A teacher? A colleague, friend, acquaintance? What were their motives in telling us this? It might have been based on care and concern, but is the result protective and helpful, or overprotective and thus unhelpful? Or, once you think it through, might control have been the motive? Or could it be based on something destructive from their own past which they are simply handing on to you, like a toxic parcel? Once you know the voice you can examine the motive behind the advice, but also if it is actually helpful to you. If it isn't, change the voice for your own, telling you something a whole lot more constructive: 'I do deserve; often this is right; mostly it is good…'.

Can you think of an example that contradicts? If you're telling yourself you can't, you shouldn't, you never…can you think of just one instance when you found your fears were not realized and this was not true? Just one? One is a crack in the dam. If you can come up with a time you managed to be skilful, if you can remember an instance when you achieved, it means the blanket belief that you 'can't' is wrong. And if you did it once you can do it again. And again.

How would it be if you could? Having looked at and examined the negatives holding you back, turn your thoughts forward. Imagine and explore what it might be like if instead of can't, oughtn't, mustn't, your motto was 'I choose to do it, I can do it and I deserve to do it…'. Each time a barrier threatens to block your way, visualize what it would feel to you and what the situation could look like if there was no barrier. Think what it would be like if you could. That's the first step towards making it happen.

GENERALIZATIONS

We all use generalizations at time – Life's A Bitch, Nothing Ever Works For Me, Teenagers Are A Pain, Men Are A Nuisance, Women Nag. We use generalizations in arguments – 'You always', 'I never', 'We regularly'. They're a useful shorthand and can let you off the hook. After all, if 'I never' or 'you always' do such-and-such, we don't have to take the responsibility for being any different. Generalizations are often self-fulfilling prophecies and tend to mean you're stuck, which is why they have no place in an assertive world. If you find yourself using one, step back and ask yourself 'Is it? Are they? Am I? And is it really always or never, everything and anything?'

Myths about who might be assertive often hold us back. We might assume that men are more assertive than women, or that assertiveness is about wealth or class and that less money or lower status means assertiveness is not for you. Looking around, it certainly seems that confidence and forcefulness goes hand in hand with being male, well off and from high status. But whatever you are born or grow up with, you can change. Assertive people are not like that because assertiveness is inborn but because they were fortunate to be trained in it. You can be retrained. Assertiveness is for all ages, both sexes and whatever life circumstances.

Essential points to consider

1   Rephrase any negative statements with positive ones.
2   Generalizations and myths can become self-fulfilling prophecies that hold you back from trying to make changes.
3   Your fear of what might happen if you seek change is usually far worse than the actuality.

Is the hard work worth it?

But is it worth it? At this point you might be feeling that it's all such hard work and futile or not worth the effort. Certainly, learning to be assertive requires effort and work and focus. But work now saves time and effort because being unassertive is actually such hard work – it's wearing and depressing and stressful. And making the leap may transform your life – yourself, your relationship and your family. The gains you will make can be apparently subtle but actually immense.

What's the worst that can happen? We often avoid facing up to painful or difficult choices because we fear what could occur if we try to change ourselves or our situation. But making the choice to do nothing is as active a decision as making the choice to do something. And the end result of doing nothing is often far more discomforting that doing something. It is the fear itself that we try to avoid.

Some years ago I read the following, from *Dune* by Frank Herbert. It's called the 'Litany Against Fear':

I must not fear.
Fear is the mind-killer.
Fear is the little-death that brings total obliteration.
I will face my fear.
I will permit it to pass over me and through me.
And when it has gone past I will turn the inner eye to see its path.
Where the fear has gone there will be nothing.
Only I will remain.

This seemed to sum up for me the struggle we all have against facing the strong emotions we have around a difficult situation, and the rewards of doing so. If you can face your fear of tackling whatever it is that makes you anxious, you may make an extraordinary discovery: that once faced, fear passes over you and leaves you confident, calm and enabled.

10 THINGS TO REMEMBER

1 *Your beliefs about yourself can hold you back.*

2 *It becomes far easier to act assertively once you have a real sense of self-worth.*

3 *You can't change other people but you can change yourself – your beliefs and the way you behave.*

4 *It can help you to examine your beliefs, and decide which you may want to discard and which to keep, if you write them down in a list.*

5 *Family, friends or other supportive people can be a great help in filling in the parts of your list you may have missed or not even be aware of.*

6 *Using negative language about yourself and your abilities can get you stuck in unhelpful patterns.*

7 *Accepting and not questioning myths and generalizations can hold you back – nearly everything can be changed if you really want to.*

8 *Assertiveness is for all ages, both sexes and most life circumstances. The gains you will make may seem subtle, but are actually immense – and you're worth it!*

9 *What's the worst that can happen? The fear of what might go wrong is what holds most of us back, yet the reality is that change can usually be good.*

10 *Frank Herbert's litany is an excellent motto. 'I will face fear... Where the fear has gone there will be nothing. Only I will remain.'*

QUIZ

1 *Are you more likely to say:*
   - **a** *I'm not bad, considering.*
   - **b** *I can't do that!*
   - **c** *I'm quite good at that, actually.*

2 *When you look in the mirror do you think:*
   - **a** *What a loser!*
   - **b** *Not bad.*
   - **c** *Hey – you're OK!*

3 *When you make a mistake do you say:*
   - **a** *Sorry – I'll do better next time.*
   - **b** *It wasn't my fault!*
   - **c** *Well, what can you expect?*

4 *Somebody offers you help, do you say:*
   - **a** *I don't need it!*
   - **b** *Oh I suppose so – go on then.*
   - **c** *Thanks!*

5 *Are your feelings about assertiveness:*
   - **a** *It's not worth all the work.*
   - **b** *It'll save so much time and effort in the future!*
   - **c** *It's hard work and taking longer than I thought.*

Scores

1a	2	3c	2
1b	1	4a	1
1c	3	4b	2
2a	1	4c	3
2b	2	5a	1
2c	3	5b	3
3a	3	5c	2
3b	1		

How did you do?

5–7 You're struggling with feeling good about yourself and managing change. Go back to the beginning and this time make sure you talk yourself through the exercises. You can do it!

8–12 You're coming along! Revise this chapter and then go on.

13–15 You have taken on board the need to change your beliefs and values. You're ready to go on to the next chapter.

6

....

Becoming assertive

In this chapter you will learn:
- *how to be SMART*
- *about the four stages of competence*
- *how to use assertiveness techniques such as 'I' messages and 'broken record'*
- *the importance of body language, words and tone*
- *about giving and receiving feedback.*

We have laid the groundwork, and established some of the ground rules, for our right to be assertive. Now we can begin practising techniques. Much of our communication is not in the meaning of the words we say but in the way the words are said and our behaviour when we say it. So we shall look at using language skills and clear communication, being direct and keeping it real, to get our points across and to build and practise our self-confidence.

Becoming assertive takes time

Becoming assertive is a process that takes time. You weren't born assertive – just needy! Some lucky people learn assertiveness as they learn to walk and talk. They learn as tiny infants that what they need will be given to them. They learn as growing toddlers that sometimes they have to wait their turn and that there are boundaries around their behaviour. Gradually, they learn if they ask firmly but also offer respect and thoughtfulness their needs will be met because they are as important as everyone else – no more, no less. But not all of us are that lucky. Many of us learn not to assert ourselves. Either we learn to fight for everything we feel we need, and become aggressive. Or we learn that it seems easier and more comfortable to knuckle under and be submissive. Or, of course, we learn to get our own way in manipulative, underhand ways.

What you're going to do now is to lose your aggression, submissiveness or passive-aggression and gain and add to the skills of assertiveness you already have. Whatever point you are at now, it helps to recognize that it will take time. It's taken you many years to reach the place you are now and while it won't take as long to unlearn lessons and take new ones on board, it will take a noticeable period. You may find yourself feeling anxious, in denial, being overwhelmed, depressed, scared, threatened or disillusioned as you make the journey. In time, you'll feel elated, capable and, finally, confident.

Insight

Becoming self-confident is the key to knowing when to assert yourself and when not. An old friend of mine has always been my model of what I think is a self-confident person. She always had an easy self-assurance that allowed her to assess a situation. At first, I thought it odd that she would occasionally let an aggressive remark or act pass without comment. Then I realized that being on the constant look out for slights and challenges makes you too quick to react. Sometimes, being self-confident means letting things go. One important aspect of assertiveness is to know how to pick your battles and recognize when to come forward and when to let it be.

5 tips to help you be assertive

► *Get on the same level when talking to someone. If they're sitting, sit down with them. If they're standing, stand up too. If it's a child, or someone in a wheelchair, crouch down.*
► *Make eye contact and be sure the person is connecting to you and the conversation by saying their name.*

- ▶ *Watch your body language. Crossing arms, hunching over and turning away all say you're defensive and not communicating. Turning towards the person, hands in lap or arms by side in a relaxed position say you're attentive. 'Mirroring' – having the same stance in reverse of the person you're talking – can send the message that you're on the same wavelength. Crowding someone by coming into their personal space is aggressive; standing your ground and allowing someone their space is assertive.*
- ▶ *If you don't feel ready to have this encounter or discussion assertively, politely but firmly suggest it be done at another time.*
- ▶ *Increase your confidence and your ability to be assertive by thinking ahead. Consider, what positive outcome can both of you achieve from this encounter?*

WHY SHOULD YOU MAKE THE TIME AND EFFORT TO LEARN ASSERTIVENESS?

Being assertive is efficient. It takes so long to beat about the bush or argue or pull strings or use any of the other tactics that are part of non-assertive behaviour. Being assertive involves a straight request or statement of needs – it gets to the point, and with care and respect.

Being assertive gives the other person their space too. They can consider your request – assertive behaviour lets other people in to make their requests or state their needs. It can give them time or room to consider, negotiate, reschedule – whatever is needed to align your needs.

Being assertive means no one has to be defensive or apologetic. It's an invitation to deal, not a demand for capitulation.

Being assertive gives everyone else a model to follow. You're being upfront, stating what you need and making it clear you would like a reply in kind. Assertive behaviour tends to trigger assertive behaviour in other people, when they see how it works. Aggression leads either to returned aggression or to capitulation and resentment; passivity to bullying and resentment; manipulation to either aggression or submission, and resentment. It's a bit like the Spam sketch from Monty Python, where everything on the menu came with spam; resentment comes with everything... except assertion.

Insight

When you're trying to make a change it can seem daunting. The scale of the task can seem so overwhelming. The trick is to understand you can't change everything overnight. Start off by changing one thing. Then another. I learnt the wisdom of breaking down tasks into small pieces many years ago when I was on holiday in Cornwall. My husband suggested we walk to the next village along a cliff path and then back along the country lanes. On the top of the first headland I realized the path stretched ahead, dipping down into tiny coves and then climbing up to more headlands, seemingly endlessly. It was miles! I couldn't walk all that! Was he mad? OK, he said, just walk down into the cove. Once there, I realized I could do the climb to the next headland. And once there, it wasn't that much of a stretch to do the next cove and maybe the next headland. Five miles later we had lunch in a picturesque village and strolled back another five miles through beautiful countryside. If I'd known at the beginning I was going to do ten miles I would almost certainly have despaired and bottled out. Bit by bit, it was easy.

Looking ahead to change

You're readying yourself to learn and practise assertiveness, and you recognize it's a process you need to work through and will take some time. It will help if you know you have to be SMART.

SMART stands for Specific, Measurable, Agreed upon, Realistic and Time-based. It's a very useful way of seeing, and remembering, what you need to do. For any change to be successful, you need to be SMART. You need to recognize that your goals should be:

S – specific. You may look at yourself and say 'I want to be better! I want to be the centre of attention, the leader of the pack, the belle of the ball!' None of that gives you an obvious pointer to what you want to be different or how you're going to do it. If, instead, you said 'I want to be able to ask my children to tidy up without it becoming an argument' or 'I want to talk to my boss and have my say without losing the thread or being interrupted' you have both a well defined and clear goal, and an indication of what you should be working on.

M – measurable. 'I want to be better!' is so vague how can you know when you have achieved it? You need to know if and when you have reached your goal and how far you need to go. So, 'I want to be able to ask my children to tidy up without it becoming an argument' or 'I want to be able to take my car to be serviced and have them do what I have asked' are measurable. You will know when you've got there.

A – agreed upon. If you're working with someone else, you have to have agreed what you're going to do, how and when by. Even with yourself, you need to come to a decision about what your goals will be, rather than slide into it in a vague, undefined manner. So agree with yourself 'Yes, what I'm going for is to be able to...' and then declare your specific, measurable goal. You could even write it down and keep it in your pocket or stuck on the fridge.

R – realistic. The worst mistake is to set the bar too high. Realistically, you're not going to go from tongue-tied silence to being able to address a meeting of two hundred people in two days. Neither can you expect to transform family mayhem into peace and love in a week. Being realistic allows you to take small steps, one at a time, to move you bit by bit from an undesirable situation to one that is better. Set realistic goals and once you have achieved one, set yourself another. Sooner or later you can look back at undreamed of changes – but you have to do them as a process, over time.

T – time-based. When you consider your specific, measurable, agreed and realistic goal you should also set a time for it to be done. This gives you an incentive to get on and do it but also allows you a reasonable period. So, 'By the end of the month I want to be able to ask my children to tidy up without it becoming an argument' or 'In ten days' time when I take my car to be serviced I want to be able to ask them to do exactly what I want.'

> ### Insight
> Setting SMART goals is obviously a business strategy but it's surprising how many skills applicable to work life function equally well in your family and personal life. And, by the way, the other way round too. All the skills you use at home – time management, negotiation and mediation, budgeting – will help you in your job. Whatever your reason for seeking assertiveness skills, it is going to benefit you all round.

The four stages of competence

Another way of making the task manageable is to see that your skills now are nothing to be ashamed of. You're at the place you are for a reason – you haven't learned better, yet. And the place you want to be is not a giant leap ahead, but a number of gradual steps. Steps you can train yourself to achieve. You can see this by considering the four stages of competence.

There are certain things we do in life that we don't have to learn. They're instinctive and automatic. Breathing is one of them. There are many other actions, however, we may think 'just come naturally' but actually have had to be learnt. You have to learn to ride a bike, drive a car, boil an egg and you may do these things with various grades of ability. You also had to learn to walk and talk, as you had to learn quite a few things you probably take for granted.

Recognizing that most of the things we take for granted needed to be learned and practised is an important stage in learning assertiveness skills. This is because all these abilities have one thing in common.

That is, you start out a total beginner and learner and end up proficient. The process from crawling to running, from not being able to cope on a mobile phone to texting your friends 20 times a day, is called the four stages of competence.

THE FIRST STAGE OF COMPETENCE

The first stage is called Unconscious Incompetence. You can't do it and don't know that you can't do it. You're lying on the floor, blowing bubbles, without realizing that hauling yourself to your feet might be both fun and an effective way of getting around. Or, you're holding this bit of plastic and metal with no idea how to use it to take or make calls. On your journey from non-assertiveness to assertiveness, at this stage you are probably losing your temper and having arguments or being put upon, and accepting that this is the way of the world.

THE SECOND STAGE OF COMPETENCE

The second stage is called Conscious Incompetence. You can't do it and you do know you can't do it. You've realized you're missing a trick – that if you could find your feet you'd get an advantage, that this chunk of plastic and metal has possibilities if only you knew how to access them. At this stage in your assertiveness journey, you realize there is a better way but can't yet manage it, and may feel frustrated and touchy that you can't.

THE THIRD STAGE OF COMPETENCE

The third stage is called Conscious Competence. You know it, and know so, but have to concentrate on what you are doing. This was the time when you were a toddler when you walked and ran but often had to watch your feet and focus on what you were doing so as not to fall. And the time you could make calls, take calls and even text but had to concentrate to get it right. In assertiveness terms, you're learning and going through the skills of being assertive, deliberately and carefully putting them into practice. And just as you fell over a lot while you were learning to walk, or miskeyed while you were learning to text, you make mistakes and fall back every so often in your assertiveness skills too.

THE FOURTH STAGE OF COMPETENCE

The fourth stage is called Unconscious Competence. You don't know you know it – it's now second nature. You walk, you run – it's as automatic as breathing. And you text with one hand while sipping a cup of coffee. Your assertiveness skills are so honed you perform them without conscious thought, automatically and easily.

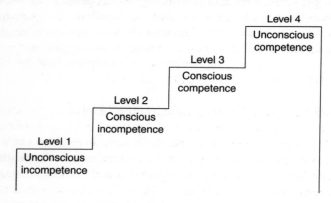

It can be really useful and confidence boosting to memorize the four stages of competence. It reminds you that being assertive is a skill you need to learn, not an art you are born knowing. It tells you that learning any skill is a process – you start off at one end and work your way towards the other. It reassures you that the reason you're having a hard time is that you are not yet at stage four, and that anyone in that situation would feel the same. And it empowers you as you recognize that you can, and will, progress up that stairway.

'I' messages

Probably the most important strategy you need to learn to become assertive is to use 'I'. Sounds odd? Sounds silly? Sounds easy? It's none of those!

We tend to be brought up to use the impersonal voice. If you think about it, how many times do you use 'you' or 'we' or 'they' or 'everyone' instead of I? As in:

'Well, you don't like to say anything, do you?'
'Sorry, we can't come.'
'They're really unhappy with you.'
'Everyone thinks you're wrong.'

We make 'You' statements for several reasons. 'Look what you made me do' or 'You make me so angry!' blame the other person for what has happened and let us off the hook. A statement such as 'Everyone thinks you're lazy' avoids taking responsibility for angry or critical remarks by saying they belong to someone else.

WHY 'YOU' STATEMENTS ARE INEFFECTIVE

The problem with 'You' statements is that they seldom give the other person a chance to understand what we're upset about, how we feel or why, or give them an opportunity to make any changes. 'You' statements may be a way of not being overwhelmed by anger or despair. Instead of 'owning' feelings, we hold them at arm's length: 'One feels like that, doesn't one?', 'That's how you do it, don't you?'

When being assertive, you need to own what you say. Instead of these roundabout ways of saying something you make it a direct statement of your own feelings or thoughts:

'I felt too embarrassed to say anything.'
'Sorry, I can't come.'
'I'm really unhappy with you.'
'I think you're wrong.'

Owning what you say is a big step since it can go against years of teaching. We're often taught as children that saying 'I' is arrogant or selfish or demanding. You might have been told 'I want doesn't get' or 'It's not all about you, you know!' The habit you might have got used to is distancing yourself from requests or comments. You don't make direct requests – I want/need/would like this – because you're afraid of showing vulnerability or of being turned down. And you don't make honest statements of how you feel – I don't like that/I don't agree with that – in case it attracts scorn or criticism, or upsets people. It can take some time to get into the habit of using 'I' statements, which isn't surprising. Most of us have had a lifetime of being told it's selfish or big-headed to say 'I'. But the more you use them, the more you'll find they work and help you and the other person feel good about the exchange.

STANDING UP FOR WHAT YOU FEEL

Being assertive is standing up for and by what you feel, think and mean. When you use an 'I' statement, you:

▶ *are aware of your own feelings and about what you want*
▶ *help other people understand what you are saying*
▶ *are clear, honest and direct*
▶ *make your point without blaming, criticizing or judging other people.*

An 'I' statement:

▶ *describes the behaviour I'm finding difficult*
▶ *says the effect it has on me*
▶ *tells the other person how I feel about it*
▶ *invites them to join me in finding a solution.*

Try this

I call it The Mantra because it should be a formula that trips off your tongue without your having to think about it and that you use all the time. When you want to make a point, say:

When... (Describe the particular situation or behaviour that is troubling you)
I feel... (Say how it makes you feel)
Because... (Say what it is about the situation or behaviour that upsets you)

TAKING RESPONSIBILITY FOR YOUR FEELINGS

'I' statements are all about being able to say what 'I want' and what 'I need'. They help the person speaking, and the person being spoken to, be clear about what is really going on. Using an 'I' statement respects the other person and their point of view. It helps you say what you feel and want but avoids making the other person feel like they're the problem. This makes it far easier for both of you to come up with a solution, take responsibility and act positively and so is essential in your quest to become assertive. Using them also puts the authentic voice into your contacts with other people.

Being open and genuine feels a very scary thing to do. Surely, you might feel, people will think worse of me if I really let them see who I am?

In fact, the result is usually the absolute opposite. Most of us have had the experience of being with someone who was frank about themselves, their abilities and skills and also their anxieties and mistakes, and we can remember how refreshing and how inspiring such people can be. One of the core skills of assertiveness is being authentic. Being authentic is about expressing who we are, what we think or feel in any situation at that moment. It is not bragging, which usually implies 'I am better than...'. Nor, if we own up to doubts, is it talking about ourselves in a way that puts ourselves down. The essential difference is that between saying 'I'm a really hopeless organizer' and 'Today I am having trouble getting everything done'. The former says 'That's what I *am* and I'm stuck with being like that' and it belittles you. The latter describes not you but your behaviour, which is temporary so you're not stuck with it.

1 *Becoming assertive takes time. It's not instinctive and needs to be learned.*
2 *Getting self-confidence is the key to knowing when to assert yourself and when not to.*
3 *Pick your battles carefully and recognize when it's worth coming forward and when it's not.*
4 *Assertiveness lets you have your say and get to the point while still having care and respect for others.*
5 *Using 'I' statements will help both you and the person you are speaking to.*

Insight

Beginning to own what we are experiencing and feeling and thinking is the place to start. We need to take notice of, listen to, and be aware of our reactions in any situation. We need to express those in a way that doesn't put them on to anyone else. So the language we use is important – using 'I' statements instead of 'one', 'you', 'they' and other generalizations.

Exercise

Here are some 'You' statements. Using the formula, can you change them into 'I' statements?

'You' statement	'I' statement
You make me so angry!	
You're so selfish.	

'You' statement	'I' statement
Look what you've made me do!	
You're acting like a baby.	
All you ever do is complain.	

Broken record

Broken record is another useful technique to make sure that you are listened to and that your message is received. Children are experts in the use of a form of broken record technique and often use it very effectively for themselves – highly exasperating for their parents.

'Broken record' refers to those old vinyl discs we used to play – you may remember them or at least have heard about them. Unlike CDs or DVDs they were quite delicate and were easily scratched or chipped. They were activated by a needle that went round a groove and when one had been damaged the needle would often skip and get stuck in a groove and keep repeating the same bit. In broken record what you do is keep repeating your point or your request until the other person recognizes and acknowledges what you are saying.

Broken record helps you to avoid being diverted or drawn into arguments. It's a technique that helps you be insistent. Sometimes when people are actively involved in their own concerns or needs they pay little attention to what you have to say or to your situation. Broken record makes sure that your message does get through without nagging, whinging or whining.

With the broken record technique it is important to use some of the same words over and over again in different sentences. This reinforces the main part of your message and prevents others raising red herrings or diverting you from your central message.

Broken record is a really important strategy for making your feelings and needs known. It's not about powering through your wishes, although sometimes it does result in not only getting across a request but encouraging the other person to change their behaviour or do something. You still may not get exactly what you want – even when you do it 'right', you may not get the 'right' response. Other people, after all, have their own thoughts and agendas, and may have their own needs and feelings to take into account. But if you're coming up against arguments for argument's sake or if others are just dragging their heels and being unreasonable, broken record demonstrates that having thought through your request and decided it is justified, you won't back down from making it. Mainly, it's a way of making sure you have your say. It's not a first strategy to employ – use it when you have asked or offered to negotiate previously and the person you're dealing with is digging in their heels.

USING BROKEN RECORD

The keys to using broken record effectively are:

- ▶ *being clear about what you want*
- ▶ *standing your ground*
- ▶ *not losing your temper*
- ▶ *making it clear that you've heard and recognized what the other person is saying to you and sympathize. Phrases to use would be 'I can see…', 'You say…', 'I realize…', 'That may be how it feels to you…'*

This is how it might work:

Istelle: Darren, it's your turn to make the meal tonight. Everything you need is in the fridge.

Darren: I've got emails to do.

Istelle:	I can see you have things you want to do, but I'd like you to start the meal now.
Darren:	I'll do it when I've finished this.
Istelle:	It's late and I'm sure you're as hungry as I am. I'd like you to do it now please while I have a bath.
Darren:	You're always nagging me!
Istelle:	I can see how you might feel I'm getting at you, but please, I want you to start the meal now.
Darren:	God, you're just doing this assertive thing at me again and I hate it!
Istelle:	That may be how it feels to you, but I'd like you to start cooking please.
Darren:	Istelle, I've had a really hard day. Can't I just have a few minutes peace and then I'll do it.
Istelle:	I realize you've had a rough day. Please make us a meal now.
Darren:	OK, OK, I'm doing it.

Be polite, don't raise your voice or lose your temper. Persist, repeating the request and go on far longer than you might think would be comfortable. If you keep it calm and don't rise to any bait or argument, you will be surprised how many times you can simply repeat a message. If you're not getting anywhere, after as many attempts as you feel able to repeat, try one final time.

'I've asked you ten times and I'd like to ask you once more to please begin cooking our meal now.'

If you then feel you are getting nowhere or are losing your cool, break off saying:

'OK, we'll leave this for ten minutes and then we'll discuss it again.'

Go away and congratulate yourself for not having lost your temper and for having left the door open for further talk. After ten minutes, go back. You may find the other person has started doing what your requested – if so, thank them without further comment. If not, resume and continue. If you do this without reproaches, complaint or threats and without getting hooked into arguing, it isn't nagging. It's making yourself clear. The other person will get the message that you're serious, won't be deflected, drawn or incited to violence (verbal or otherwise) and will persist. Sooner or later, they are likely to co-operate.

The importance of tone

Paying attention to what we say isn't enough. How you say it is actually even more significant. Here's an easy way to recognize the importance of how we put our ideas across. Think about the way people tell jokes or funny stories. One person can have you rolling on the floor with a joke or a story. But another person can tell exactly the same anecdote or gag with no effect whatsoever. What's going on? Well, according to quite a few studies, meaning isn't only in what we actually say. Less than 10 per cent of what we convey comes across in the words alone. Over a third is 'paralinguistic' – that means, the tone or way things are said. Consider this statement, said to a teenager passing through the kitchen, ready for a night out with her friends: 'You're going out in that.'

Using the word 'that' already implies a criticism (that rag, that costume, that skimpy bit of nonsense) but said with equal emphasis on all words – 'You're going out in that' – it at least comes over as a fairly neutral question.

Said with extreme emphasis on 'you're' – *'you're* going out in that' – it becomes 'With homework and chores not yet done? Dream on!'

Said with extreme emphasis on 'out' – 'You're going *out* in that' – it becomes 'You can wear what you like at home but don't you dare show me up in public dressed in such a way!'

Said with extreme emphasis on 'that' – 'You're going out in *that*' – it becomes 'Over my dead body my girl – what a mess, you look like a tart!'

Varying degrees of disgust, sarcasm, scorn and anger in your voice transforms a simple statement into confrontation – angry words, slammed doors, tears. Mumbling, stumbling, using too may 'ums', 'ahs' and 'ers', peppering your speech with 'you know', 'like' and 'innit', can dilute the strength of what you want to say or even change the meaning. Using slang and the sort of short-cut references that come from having shared jokes or seen the same films and TV shows can help when talking with family, friends or close colleagues but may not work when used with people from another generation or in a formal setting. Approach your boss and say 'Umm, er, what I want to ask, if you don't mind, I mean, it's like, you know, I'd sort of like a pay rise' would have a very different result from saying 'Can we talk? I've been looking at what I've been doing for the company lately and in the light of new responsibilities and productivity I'd like us to discuss an increase in my salary'. The reverse can also be true: using very formal or elaborate language out of place can be just as unhelpful.

Insight

I belong to a writing group and we have a joke about the term 'floral tributes'. 'Floral tributes' is my term for not calling a spade a spade – it's using words far too elaborate for the use you make of them. You might take a floral tribute to a funeral. At all other times, you have flowers. Using inappropriate language is the sort of thing you do when you feel nervous or awkward. And using it both makes you nervous and awkward and shows how uneasy you feel. Being assertive and being real go hand in hand. If you make the effort to say it like it is, not how you might think it should be said, you'll find yourself becoming more assertive.

BREATHING AND TALKING

It's a good idea to practise how to breathe and talk. Yes, I know you've been doing the first since you were born and the second since you were two – but that's plenty of time to pick up some bad habits!

Breathing is often the key to whether you feel assertive or not, and whether you sound assertive or not. When we feel nervous and under stress, breathing often quickens sometimes even to the point of hyperventilating or overbreathing. This can cause you to feel unsteady, light-headed and dizzy. And, of course, out of control of the situation and yourself, self-conscious and severely lacking in self-confidence. Not assertive at all, in other words! When you're breathing too quickly your voice may also go wobbly or high, further showing how anxious you feel, and denting your self-confidence further. Consciously slowing your breathing when you feel nervous and under stress can help you calm down.

Try this

It only takes a few moments to relax and bring your breathing, and yourself, under control. If you have the opportunity, lie down with some music. Even if you can't lie down and have no music, you can still do the following. Breathe deeply and let your breath out slowly. Focus your mind on something you find soothing – an image of the sea or a quiet wood, wind blowing through grass or somewhere you feel safe such as your bedroom. Imagine yourself there and see, hear, taste, smell and feel it. Count your breaths slowly in and out, reassuring yourself that you can relax and manage. After a minute or so, take another deep breath, let it out slowly and come back to the real world, with your breathing now normal and yourself calm.

WATCHING YOUR TONE AND PITCH

In relearning how to talk, you focus on your tone and pitch. If you listen to how the people you like or trust or respect talk, you can pick up tips on how you can do it too. Range and variety are important. Talking all on one level sounds monotonous and boring, and also makes you appear nervous. Listen to how you talk when you're with people with whom you feel comfortable. Your voice is likely to be warmer, more animated, with far more ups and downs and variations. Then listen to yourself when you're feeling threatened. Voices tend to go up in pitch and to flatten out when we're unsure. Pitching your voice down low, so it conveys warmth and control rather than nervousness, can make a difference not only to how others see you, but to how you see yourself. This is not about changing your accent or 'learning how to speak proper'; it's about being yourself but with self-confidence.

Practice makes perfect. Initially, practise in your mind and imagine yourself using 'I' statements or responding to other people's attempts at dominating or manipulating you. Visualize yourself behaving in a firmer manner, saying firmer things, asking firm, clear, probing questions, and presenting well-prepared facts and evidence. What you will be doing is re-conditioning yourself, gradually, from responding either with 'Yes, of course!' or 'Oh dear, it's all too much!' or 'Don't talk to me like that!' to more effective reactions.

Responses you could use might be:

- ▶ *I need to think that over. I'll come back to you.*
- ▶ *If you want an answer now it's no. If we can talk this over and I have time to think about it, it might be different.*
- ▶ *Yes, I can do that, but I will need more information/time to make arrangements/some support.*
- ▶ *No, I can't do that.*
- ▶ *I'd be happy to help but not today. Tomorrow/next Thursday/ next week is good.*

Practise your skills with yourself – use a mirror so you can get an idea of how you look. Even better, use a webcam or camera or mobile phone so you can play it back and see yourself exactly as others see you. Yes, it's embarrassing. Yes, you might feel silly. Get over it! Learn how to put your feelings and needs on the agenda, on the same level as the people asking you to do something. Remind yourself, constantly, that you are as important as they are – no more but no less. They may need you to do something for them. Fine. You may need NOT to do that thing. It's up to you to prioritize these needs but just as they will be looking after themselves, you should look after yourself.

The importance of body language

And it isn't just the words and the tone in which we say things that adds to either our meaning or the understanding of the recipient. You also need to factor in our facial expressions and our body language. These have been shown to account for over 50 per cent of meaning in our communication.

Said with a lifted eyebrow as a gentle question 'You're going out in that?' becomes 'Well, it might look fine but it's quite cold – wouldn't leggings be more appropriate?'

Said with pursed lips it becomes 'You look awful!'

Said with a curled lip it becomes 'You look so awful words cannot describe my horror.'

Body language describes the way you hold yourself and it too sends messages independent of the words you are using. Five important body postures are mirroring, congruence, incongruence, closed position and open position.

MIRRORING

Mirroring is when you find yourself copying the stance of the person with whom you are talking – crossing your legs or leaning forward when they do as if you were mirror images of each other. You may not realize you are doing it and neither may the other person, but the likely effect is that both of you will feel you are in tune with each other and on the same wavelength. If you want to reassure and give confidence to someone while you are talking, this is a good way to do it. It can also be felt by the other person to mean you are in a submissive position, following their lead and doing what they choose to do. You can consciously use mirroring to instil reassurance and confidence. Used with assertion it does not appear slavish but conveys the message that you are listening.

CONGRUENCE

Congruence is when your body language and your facial expressions match the words you are using. So, if you are happy and amused you'd be smiling; if serious or even unhappy, you would be solemn.

INCONGRUENCE

Incongruence is when your body language and your facial expressions do not match the words you are using. You may be angry or upset but smiling. You may be making a complaint, but by avoiding eye contact and crossing your arms or huddling you send out the message that you feel vulnerable and defensive.

The dangers of incongruence

When you say 'I'm really upset with you' but smile as you say it, or turn away to hide or avoid eye contact, this totally undercuts your words. We often do this because we're nervous and scared of the other person's reaction, or because we feel being nice while delivering criticism or complaint will prevent conflict. But the effect is not to lower the tension or deflect an angry response, it is to absolutely sabotage what you're trying to say. If your body language, your tone and your words don't match up, it doesn't make your message any more palatable, it simply causes confusion. An important aspect of assertiveness, then, is congruency – when what you say and how you say it match.

CLOSED POSITION

Closed position is when you cross arms and legs, or make sure there is a barrier between you and the person you are talking to – a cushion, an article of clothing, a table. The message this body position sends is that you feel under threat. The more you entwine your limbs or huddle inwards and avoid eye contact, the more defensive you appear.

OPEN POSITION

Open position is when you stand or sit upright with arms held loosely, in your lap or by your side, with your legs uncrossed. This pose sends the message that you are open and receptive, confident and secure.

Our physical presence powerfully sets the scene for our emotional state. Making eye contact, using a warm and low tone of voice, making gestures with our hands and arms that take up space but do not crowd or impose on others all tell people we feel self-confident and have self-esteem and a sense of self-worth.

BODY LANGUAGE SENDS OUT POWERFUL MESSAGES

It's interesting that this confidence and sense of self-worth can be felt by others seeing you in a very short time and in all sorts of circumstances, and the results can be startling. Some years ago in a study on body language, people in prison for crimes against persons, such as mugging and assault, were shown a series of pictures and asked which people shown in these they would have picked as victims. The same people were repeatedly chosen and it was those who projected uncertainty, whose body language was apologetic, defensive and submissive. Those who showed authority, confidence and certainty in the way they walked and stood were generally not chosen as likely victims. Walking tall works.

PRACTISING BODY LANGUAGE

So how can you put into practice using body language to go with your new use of 'I' statements? Consider these scenarios and think about how your initial temptation might be to react:

▶ *A workmate who sucks their teeth and whistles, putting you off, tells you they've been told they're annoying. They ask you if you agree.*
▶ *Your teenager leaves the kitchen in a mess. You're about to speak with them when you realize they're in a really bad mood.*
▶ *You and your partner go out for a meal and sit opposite each other across a table.*
▶ *You meet someone new at a party and take an instant liking to them.*
▶ *You meet someone new at a party and take an instant dislike to them.*
▶ *You take a pair of shoes back to the shop – the heel came off the first time you wore them.*

Did you mirror the person you were talking to? Use open or closed position? Were you congruent? What do you think your tone of voice and body language might have revealed about your feelings, about them and the situation? What do you think might be the result of your body language, your tone and the words and the emphasis you might have chosen to use?

Now, do the exercise again. This time, imagine yourself using all the techniques we have so far discussed – 'I' messages, using body language and voice modulation – to be effective. Could you see how being confident and authoritative when necessary, using techniques that say 'We're very alike' or 'I'm open to what you say to me' when appropriate, could smooth your communication with others?

Resisting pressure

What if you're anxious – perhaps from experience – that the other person may shout or otherwise put unpleasant pressure on you? Again, practise the situation and your response, until you realize it really doesn't hurt – it just makes the person doing the shouting look stupid. Do it to yourself in that mirror or camera. Get a friend or family member to really let rip, shouting right in your face, or to whine and wheedle. Think of the things that frighten or influence you – being told 'Do what I say!'; 'Are you stupid or what?'; 'How many times must I tell you?'; 'You'll be sorry when I'm gone!'; 'It's not too much to ask, is it?' or 'Just this once, you owe it to me.' Do it, again and again, each time say calmly 'You don't frighten me, you don't get to me.' The trick is not to be drawn in to answering what the other person is shouting or saying – simply to remind yourself, and them, that it doesn't have the desired effect which is to cow, frighten and force you to do what they want. Practise it until you can control your response to being shouted at or manipulated.

The fact is that the biggest tantrum and the most practised whine is no match for a well-organized defence. Once you are convinced of your own rights and have used some assertiveness techniques you can use them to defend and support your position.

It's worth considering that the very explosion in new ways of getting and keeping in touch can make true communication harder. Emails, social networking sites, twitters – all have one thing in common: they remove over 90 per cent of our ability to communicate fully, by taking facial expression and tone out of the equation. All you have is the words – and words can seem brisk, bald and cold when you can't hear or see someone saying them.

A quick note – I can't come tonight/thanks for that/see you soon – may be taken by you as simply informational. But you may, equally, feel slighted or hurt or shaken or puzzled if you can't hear someone's regret or apology or sincerity when they deliver it. Our knowledge of assertive techniques can also be used to recognize when the extra word or two in a message or email might soften it so that our true meaning comes across.

Insight

Keep in mind that when someone wants to dominate or manipulate you, they are the ones with the problem, not you. They want something from you – to do something for them or simply to validate their need to be in control. Being unassertive means giving in to their needs over your own. But it means you have to give over that control – hand it over like a parcel. It may feel as if it's snatched from your hands and you can't keep hold. Or that it really belongs to them and they have the right to demand it. The truth is it's your parcel, not theirs. You can keep hold because they can't take it from you unless you consent.

Essential points to consider

1 *Your actual words and the tone you use are all-important. As are your facial expression and body language – they are over 50 per cent of your meaning in communication.*
2 *Learn to recognize and use mirroring, congruence, incongruence and open and closed positions.*
3 *Pay attention to the tone and pitch of your voice.*
4 *Practise the suggested relaxation and breathing techniques to help you stay in control in any situation.*
5 *Once you have convinced yourself of your rights and you have mastered some assertiveness techniques, you should be able to support your position at all times.*

Having reasonable expectations

You need to have reasonable expectations about yourself and about your progress in becoming assertive. You can't become totally confident overnight. It takes practice to become focused, relaxed, serene, calm and firm. One thing you may need to become skilled at is stilling the small, secret voice that tells you that you can't do it. You can practise broken record on other people. You should also sometimes do it to yourself.

> **Insight**
> Small steps are best. You can feel overwhelmed by the changes you may have to make and expect yourself to move mountains at once. Remember it took you ages to get where you are now and it may take some time to get to where you want to be. You'll do it, if you can recognize you'll do it bit by bit, one step at a time.

Sit down and think for a moment what circumstances you find hard, and what you might be telling yourself (or remembering other people telling you) you can't do. For instance:

Don't be silly – you can't do that!
You'll never manage!
People like us aren't supposed to do that!

Fill in your own:

Now, for each negative thought come up with an affirmative one:

Don't be silly – you can't do that!	Of course I can do it.
You'll never manage!	I know I can manage that.
People like us aren't supposed to do that!	I can do that – I have the same rights as anybody.

Fill in your own:

(Contd)

Choosing priorities

Being assertive sometimes means acting and sometimes means choosing to step aside. In some circumstances, you'll need to speak up and not let your rights and your dignity be trampled. Sometimes, you achieve as much by knowing when to leave it. For instance – somebody tries to queue jump, you can, and should, object. 'Excuse me – I was here first. Your place is back there.' But if someone in front of you in the queue seems to be taking an excessive length of time, however much you may be in a hurry, it's not your right to object to that. You should have made more time yourself – bite on it.

In seeking respect for yourself you also have to respect others. Being assertive means claiming your place beside everyone else. It does not mean fighting to be top of the heap over everyone else. It's worth always asking yourself which you'd regret more – speaking out or leaving well alone. If you know you're going to walk away seething if you don't say anything – such as when someone pushes in front of you and you don't intervene – then you know you should say so. But if your action, such as dressing someone down, would actually, on reflection, leave a nasty taste in your mouth choose to let it go.

In choosing your priorities you might also take a lateral approach. For instance, a family member drives you crazy by forgetting to use a clean knife or a spoon in the butter or honey and always leaves crumbs. Maybe you've tried 'I' messages and broken record and it still seems to happen. You want to have crumb-free butter and honey but do you really want to go on making this so important?

So go lateral. Buy a second pack of butter and jar of honey. Label them 'Crumb-free – use a clean knife, use the other one or die'.

Case study

Dot and Raymond seemed to have endless arguments with their children over doing one particular chore – the washing up. After Dot had used the techniques she'd learned to ask them to help round the house they'd do anything else – feed the dog, tidy up and even vacuum their own and family rooms – but washing up was their pet hate and they'd all fight and row over whose turn it was. Last Christmas, Dot was given a work bonus and went straight out with it and bought a dishwasher. The children vied with each other to fill it and even accepted emptying it. But with no more washing up, peace reigned.

Making decisions

Making decisions is about choosing between one course of action and another. We often find it hard to prioritize and say '*This* is what I will do, *that* is what I will not do' because it seems so final and momentous. And of course if we've decided, we're then responsible for what happens. It feels as if when we don't decide but let it happen, we can't be held accountable. But you need to remind yourself that when you leave things to take their course, that in itself is a decision to act. You are really just as liable for a decision taken passively as you are for one you actively settle on.

Life tends to be a succession of big and small decisions. Latte or cappuccino? A chocolate biscuit or a plain one? Shall I go for these qualifications? Should we marry or live together? Take this job? Negotiate this home? Sometimes, we stress over an apparently small one and make a snap choice over a large one – the committee equivalent of taking an hour to decide what colour to paint the bike shed and two minutes to agree a multi-million deal. Being assertive is recognizing that it's the process of making a decision that is the important step. Whether the decision is big or small, making a choice is the same; it's about acknowledging that you have the right to say yea or nay, this or that. And that you are prepared to then live with your choice – or change it if necessary. You are in control, and happy to be so. And in taking control, you also acknowledge that while the process is the same, not all decisions are as important as others. Which is why you can dig in your heels about some, but let others go.

PRIORITIZING YOUR DECISIONS

It's worthwhile putting any choice to a test:

Why might I go one way or another? Are you inclined for or against because of the greater good of everyone involved? Or are you biased one way because you want to please someone, are afraid of a reaction, or are being influenced by something in your past?

How long will this decision live with me? However it feels, an argument over which programme to watch on TV is not important; you may have a passing regret if around the water cooler next day you have to say 'I didn't see it', but an hour later, it really won't matter. So don't fight over the TV remote the way you might over a decision to move house.

Who else is affected by my decision? Demanding you always get your way may have lasting effects on those around you, leading them to resent you, or spend time away, shunning you. Others always being allowed to have their own way, on the other hand, sets up a situation where you become the doormat, seething in resentment while they never have to learn to compromise or think of others. Balance up your needs against other people's – neither should always take priority.

A small decision can become a big one. Who gets the TV remote and a choice of programmes can, if it always goes one way, end up with a family split down the middle and hardly communicating. While a big one – such as what exams to take – can become less significant when you can revisit and renegotiate.

Sandy's wife Bev always regretted not getting professional
qualifications. She'd wanted to be a social worker but had fallen
pregnant while still at school and Sandy had put pressure on her
to leave and get married. Bev worked as a home carer and when
their younger son began secondary school her boss suggested she
do an Open University course for a social work degree. Sandy was
obstructive and critical at first but Bev's growing confidence and
skills helped her talk it over with him and address the insecurities
which were at the bottom of his anxieties over her advancement.
Sandy worked in a bank and a year after Bev started her degree,
he finally gave in to her reassurance and his own boss's urging and
began studying for accountancy qualifications.

Rewards

One way to make sure you keep on the little by little, gradual
steps towards being confident and assertive is to reward yourself,
regularly. You make small gains and small victories all the time and
the more you recognize that, the higher will be your esteem and
the better you will perform. Give yourself small rewards – a cup
of coffee, a few minutes with your feet up listening to some music,
a night in or out seeing a film of your choice. Frequent, regular
rewards will remind you that you slowly build towards your goal.
At the end of a few months or even a year you can look back, and
reward yourself for the continued progress you have made.

Essential points to consider

1 *Use 'broken record' to make sure you are listened to
and your message is received.*
2 *Realistic expectations are more effective than trying to
change everything overnight.*

(Contd)

3 *Knowing when to leave well alone is sometimes as*
  valuable as knowing when to jump in.
4 *Life is usually a succession of big and small decisions.*
  Recognizing that it is the process of making these choices
  that is the important step is one of the keys of assertiveness.
5 *Give yourself regular small rewards for achieving*
  small goals.

Assertive people aren't assertive all the time

Don't berate yourself for getting it wrong. Assertive people aren't
assertive all the time. They can lose it under pressure, especially
with those nearest and dearest, and shout at partners and kids
and parents. But the key to assertiveness is knowing how it could
be done, doing it as often as possible and when you screw up,
recognizing so, apologizing and offering redress.

Here is a useful formula for acting assertively:

- *Put your finger on what you want done.*
- *Say how you feel.*
- *Explain why you want it done, and how it fits in.*
- *Get agreement.*
- *Say thanks!*

You're faced with this situation: you've come home late, because
of heavy traffic. You want to get the evening meal ready quickly,
a family member is there watching TV and you need some help.
If you're having a bad day and your skills have temporarily
deserted you, this is how it might go:

Lenny: Dan, don't just sit there you lazy so-and-so. Get off
        your backside and empty the dishwasher.
Dan: I did it yesterday! It's not my turn!
Lenny: I don't give a damn. I've got enough on my plate – you
        really get on my nerves!

Dan:	I've got stuff to do and anyway, you're always on at me!
Lenny:	I'm on at you because you never help unless I shout at you.
Dan:	That's so unfair – I did it yesterday.
Lenny:	Look, just do it, OK?
Dan:	P*** off – I'm going out!

Take a deep breath, and begin again.

Lenny:	Dan, I'm sorry about that. I shouldn't have shouted at you, I've had a bad day. I'd like you to empty the dishwasher of yesterday's dishes and fill it with this morning's, and lay the table.
Dan:	I told you – I did it yesterday! It's not my turn!
Lenny:	I need some help because I'm running behind – the bus was late. And I'd like to get the evening meal ready. I'm feeling really tired and hungry and I'm sure you are too. With your help, I can get our meal on the table as soon as possible.
Dan:	Oh, well... all right.
Lenny:	Thanks – that's a great help!

Being liked and being assertive

Insight

You don't have to choose between being liked and being assertive. If it seems that way, what you're actually choosing is between asserting yourself, or being the easy one who can always be dumped on. Nobody actually likes a doormat because real liking entails respect.

You can be firm – really, really firm – without being aggressive. The key is to have your focus fixed on getting a solution, having your say and hearing the other person's view too. Whether this is someone you see every day or someone you encounter once, the outcome you want to achieve is to make a difference and to have a lesson learnt. You can't do that if you are submissive or aggressive. Neither can you do it if your main aim is to be liked or to have an easy time. Sometimes, you and another person dislike each other and will always do so. Accept it and learn to work with it. Don't be needy – it's dangerous because it leads you to make decisions that run counter to being assertive. An important step to being assertive is accepting that sometimes it means people are upset. What you need to decide is who would you rather was upset – you, because you're treated like a doormat and never get what you need or want? Or occasionally other people, because you step up and expect to get what you deserve?

Case study

Ayesha acknowledged that she let her children walk all over her. Every night was a battle over bedtimes and she was forever having to write notes to their teachers excusing forgotten homework. At least once a week one or other of them would leave their school lunch behind and she'd be late for work having driven out of her way to drop it off. She finally realized she couldn't take it anymore and contacted me. When we talked, she was able to see her main wish was for her children to like her, because as she tearfully admitted, she hadn't liked her own mother. Ayesha remembered endless rules and regulations throughout her childhood and didn't want to visit that on her own children. What she eventually realized was that she hadn't disliked her mother because of the rules she laid down but because of the absence of love and affection and of any sort of flexibility. She came to see her children needed her love but they also needed some tough love. Parents aren't friends, to be liked because they never hold you to account and make things easy for you, but adults who take responsibility for your well-being. Ayesha started holding the boundaries – explaining some rules such as bedtimes and doing homework in time, with sanctions such as no TV or having to be home early if the children didn't comply. It led to more arguments at first. And then, it led to discussions and agreement. It took some weeks but what became clear was that her children actually felt more secure and happier when she was an adult and parent rather than trying to make them like her as if she was their friend by not having or applying sensible rules.

In some cases, you may have to accept that nothing you do is going to change the other person. For whatever reason, either they can't get it or won't get it. Whatever, the truth is that you can never change someone else: they have to want to change themselves. In which case, the trick is to make your statement so that you have the satisfaction of having been assertive, and move on. Who knows – by saying your piece and letting go you may leave behind you a ticking time bomb so that someday they say 'Oh. Now I get it.'

Using 'What we're going to do is...'

When you use the 'Put your finger on what you want done; Say how you feel; Explain why you want it done, and how it fits in; Get agreement; Say thanks!' formula, there is another phrase you can sometimes use as well to get things done. This is 'What we're going to do is...'.

It's a very useful statement. It tells the other person what you want to happen. It doesn't complain or criticize or judge the past performance, but simply lays out a plan of action. Depending on the circumstances you might like to add 'What do you think?' so the other person can put up their own ideas for negotiation. But in the situation I've suggested (and I've used the name Suzie for a reason...) being firm is the name of the game: you know what you want and that is what is going to happen.

You put your car in to have the air conditioner fixed. The car comes back and the first time you turn on the air con, it clearly isn't working. You take it back to the garage. It could go like this:

Suzie:	I brought this car in to have the air conditioner fixed and it's still not working.
Mechanic:	It was working when we finished with it.
Suzie:	Well, it isn't working now!
Mechanic:	It was working when it left us.

Suzie:	Are you saying I broke it?
Mechanic:	All I'm saying is it's down on the job sheet as working when we finished it.
Suzie:	It's not working! What are you going to do about it?
Mechanic:	We can book it in again.
Suzie:	What, and charge me again?
Mechanic:	It was working when we'd finished with it.

Or, it can go like this:

Suzie:	I brought this car in to have the air conditioner fixed and it's still not working.
Mechanic:	It was working when we'd finished with it.
Suzie:	When I used it first time, it wasn't working. What we're going to do is you're going to take the car back and complete the job so it works when I use it too. Do you need me to talk to the manager to clear you to do this within the original invoice?

Then, either:

| Mechanic: | No, that won't be necessary. Perhaps we missed something. I'll get the diary. |

Or:

Mechanic:	It was working when it left us.
Suzie:	Fine. I'll talk to the manager. OK, as I was telling your mechanic, I brought this car in to have the air conditioner fixed and when I used it first time, it wasn't working. According to him it was working when they had finished but I'm not really interested in that. It should work when I use it. What we're going to do is you're going to take the car back and complete the job so it works when I use it too.
Manager:	Of course. I do apologize. Let's get the diary and book you in.
Suzie:	Thank you, I appreciate that.

Dealing with unpleasant situations

How do you deal with racism, sexism, snide comments, complaints about your spouse or children, from people you know, or don't know? These are perhaps the most common issues that lead people to realize they could do with help in being assertive. It can feel harder to deal with such concerns when it's with someone you know, or have to go on dealing with, such as a relative, a friend or acquaintance, or a work colleague. But using assertiveness strategies, we can put our point of view across and stop the behaviour – or at least feel we have regained some control of the situation.

Racism, sexism, and this sort of unpleasant meanness tends to be a way for people to gain the upper hand. By labelling and putting down other people, they seek to make themselves feel superior or powerful. Sometimes, all that is needed to stop harassment is to challenge it, because in doing so you show you aren't as powerless as the other person thought.

Case study

A new manager joined Dawn's workplace and within a few days began calling her 'Darling', 'Honey' and 'Sweetie'. Dawn let it go for two days and then, when he came into the room and greeted her with 'Morning, darling' she looked him straight in the eyes and said 'My name is Dawn. Since this is a workplace and we

(Contd)

need to deal with each other with mutual trust and respect I'd like you to remember that.' He looked startled and began to say 'Look, I'm only being friendly...' and she just shook her head and repeated firmly 'This is a workplace. My name is Dawn.' He acted appropriately after that. Simply taking the initiative redrew the boundaries and put him on warning.

If someone says something you really disagree with or find offensive, you can:

- *quietly put your view: say 'No, that's not the way I see it'*
- *quietly challenge it: say 'I disagree and I'm uncomfortable with that comment/language.' You could add 'That's unacceptable/that's rude/that hurts. I don't appreciate comments like that. I don't want to hear that again'*
- *absent yourself: sometimes, simply walking away sends a powerful message that you aren't going to join in or be an audience to such sentiments.*

If the person argues, remember broken record:

- *'It doesn't matter if you think what you said/did was OK, I don't. Please don't do it again.'*
- *'It doesn't matter/I don't care if no one else has ever objected, I'm objecting. Please don't do it again.'*
- *'It doesn't matter if you think everyone else finds it acceptable, I don't. Please don't do it again.'*

Insight
Make a smile something that projects friendliness and a willingness to negotiate – *not* a desire to conciliate or back down.

Giving and receiving feedback

Another technique that can help in becoming assertive is that of giving and receiving feedback. Feedback means the process of giving and receiving information about behaviour in a particular situation. You can give feedback about another person's behaviour to them and then they can give you feedback on your own. You can also give feedback on your own behaviour, and listen to theirs on themselves, and then discuss your reactions with each other.

Giving and receiving feedback is useful for several reasons:

▶ *It tells you what you are doing and how you are coming across to others. You can learn from this to amend and change your behaviour if necessary.*
▶ *It can give you an insight into how you behave. Other people can often see aspects of us which we cannot see ourselves. We can particularly be blinded by a culture which tends to put people down, and teaches us to put ourselves down. If your head is full of self-critical messages, such as 'I can't really do that', 'Nobody will listen to me', 'What I think doesn't matter' you may miss what you are doing right – which someone else can see.*
▶ *Very often, it is easier to see the special qualities and uniqueness of others than it is to see your own. Exchanging feedback means you can help someone else by speaking out about their strengths, and they can do the same for you.*

When giving and receiving feedback it's often useful to use these two questions:

▶ *What did I/they do well?*
▶ *What could I/they do differently?*

It is far more effective to think about what you could have done differently than what you think you might have done wrong. We tend to be self-critical and focus on our mistakes, which can actually lock you into a self-fulfilling cycle; you think about what you did wrong and so keep repeating it, unable to see another option. That doesn't help when you are usually doing the best you can and what you need is a boost to learn from what happens and take it a step further. So, start by being reminded of how well you did, by someone else and yourself. Once you have heard this and taken it in, it is much more likely that you will be able to hear and use the comments about how you might change.

HOW TO GIVE FEEDBACK

Feedback should always be:

Specific. Rather than being told 'you are terrific', it is good to hear exactly what you did or said, or how you were, that made you so effective. 'You were so friendly and kind with that salesperson – it really made him go the extra mile for us.'

Descriptive. The more detail that you can say in answer to what you thought someone did well or could have done differently, the more resource of information the recipient has to draw on and learn from. It is not helpful to get into judgemental, evaluative, and critical comments. 'You'd washed up the cups and put them away. You left the wet drying up cloth on the table.'

Directed towards behaviour that can change. So, comments on someone's height, for example, which is not something that can be changed, are not helpful. But saying 'When you stand up straight you present an imposing figure – I feel I should look up to you' may help someone who is shy about their height and tends to hunch up.

Provided straight after the given behaviour. Feedback has most impact when you can link it with what you did or said. So it's best when it's fresh in your mind.

Insight

There are lots of situations in life, as a parent, a colleague or a friend, when this model of feedback is useful. It can be applied to any situation when we want our own or others' behaviour to change. Giving and receiving feedback is one of the main ways of bringing about change in people. It is a skill which deserves to be valued.

WHY FEEDBACK SHOULD NOT BE JUDGEMENTAL

Often, as we give and receive feedback, feelings come up for us. All of us have been criticized a lot in our lives, which has left us with old hurts: that others misunderstood us, didn't see the value of us, or what we were doing, and fear that we may be criticized again. This is why feedback shouldn't be critical – 'You should have hung the towel up!' or use labels 'You were so messy!' but a simple description, or a statement of what could be different – 'Having put the cups away you could hang the towel up after.'

The problem is, in our society we're used to being put down, and to putting ourselves down. We tend to expect criticism and know how to give it, but be surprised by compliments and have no idea how to deliver them. In fact, we think that anybody speaking out about our brilliance and abilities or acknowledging their own is making fun of us, 'going over the top', or faking it. We'll look later in more detail at the issues of giving criticism and accepting compliments.

The importance of choosing your arena

When you're beginning to put assertiveness techniques into action and change the way you are going to behave, it helps to choose your arena. Ask yourself, where do you find it hardest or easiest to be assertive? Hard or easy, either may be at home, or at work or in public with people you don't know. If you find it difficult to be assertive at home you may find it easier at work. If you find it hard to be assertive at home and work you may find it easier with your friends. If you find it hard there too, it's time to look for somewhere where you can be confident enough to practise these strategies. How about joining a class to learn or enjoy a hobby? By going into a completely new situation with new people who have no expectations of you, you may find you can go there with the assertiveness techniques you know about and want to put into use.

Work out what makes you feel good about yourself and confident. For some, it might be looking groomed and smart, with new clothes. For others it might be being comfortable, in casual clothes. You might be someone who feels best when you can take the initiative, or prefer being able to hang back until you have assessed the situation. You may feel better when you're going somewhere knowing all about whatever situation you're going into, or someone who likes to pick it up as you go along. Whatever suits you best, once you know, maximize the opportunities for being in your safe zone.

When you're looking to put these skills into practice, look for ways to gain skills and become comfortable with the ways and means of becoming and being more assertive. It helps to use any way to raise your self-esteem. The better you feel about yourself, the more capable and confident you will become. Look for the things you enjoy and are good at, and then push the boundary a bit. Do you have an interest you can develop – crafts, cooking, speaking a foreign language? What are you like at public speaking, acting or otherwise performing? Are you fit – would focussing on walking, jogging and eventually running or going to a gym or swimming pool not only help your health but also help make you feel positive and worthwhile? Sit down and try this exercise. Fill in as many things as you can think of in the 'What am I good at?' and 'What do I like doing?' boxes. Then, consider what you could add beside each listing to make yourself feel even better:

	How could I take that one step further?
What am I good at?	

What do I like doing?	

BEING ASSERTIVE WITH FAMILY

For many of us, it's in the family that we feel most hard done by and in the family where we are most in need of assertiveness skills. Yet while we may see the sense and take the step of learning how to stand up for ourselves in work or in public, it's often in the family where we feel awkward at making changes. Partly that's because we fear being ridiculed the most. When I began using these skills, having learned them while training to be a Relate counsellor, my stepson would cry 'Don't you try those counsellor tricks on me!' and my husband would respond to any thanks or appreciation by saying 'That sounds so odd! You don't have to thank me!' Family can have a way of being far more personally critical and even abusive than friends, colleagues or strangers. Since, however, it is the family that is often the breeding ground for bad habits, it's often the best place to start, and the most important place to learn, practise and perfect those skills. We'll look in more detail at how your changes can affect others in a later chapter, but for now it's worth laying down some ground rules for dealing with children and partners, parents and in-laws. You will need to:

- ▶ *model what you want*
- ▶ *be side by side rather than in opposition*
- ▶ *reinforce good behaviour, not bad*

Model what you want. If you want your family to be assertive rather than doormats or aggressors, you need to model it to them. You need to walk the talk, and that sometimes means getting tough with them. It means gaining the skills and going through the techniques and strategies, just as you are doing or learning how to do with anyone and anywhere else. You need to use 'I' messages, broken record and learn not to pull punches or lessen their impact. I might have got 'Don't you try those counsellor tricks on me!' and 'That sounds so odd! You don't have to thank me!' at first. Far more quickly than I had expected, I got 'Oh. Alright. Fine!' and 'Hey – I see what you mean, it does sound nice to be thanked!' And not too much longer after that, I began to see all those techniques coming back at me – people being clear, saying what they wanted and how they felt, and showing appreciation.

Be side by side rather than in opposition. In several recent reports on child happiness, one issue that was highlighted was how often children were able to say their parents talked with them. In the UK and USA, which both had astoundingly bad scores, children said the most frequent interaction between parent and child was for the parent to be criticizing and telling them off. In countries such as Norway and the Netherlands, which came out very well for childhood happiness, children said their parents would often 'just chat' and show an interest. One way of looking at it is to consider whether you see yourself side by side with, or in opposition to, your children. Are you walking up the hill with them, holding hands and chatting happily? Or are you dragging them along or driving them ahead of you? The assertive model is side by side. So is the happy one! In the end, it's far more important that you and your family enjoy each other's company than the place runs on clockwork. The dust comes back tomorrow – an alienated child or spouse may not. Which of the following is likely to get a better response?

Hi! Tell me about your day!	Oh, you're here. Um, yes. Er – did you do well at school today?
That looks awful, wherever did you get that?	You look dramatic/colourful/interesting.
Oh, what a mess.	I'll give you a hand to finish the washing up.
You did all that clearing up and hung up your clothes!	(nothing said)
Oh for heaven's sake, get on with it!	Come and share a coffee with me.
How did your project go? I've been thinking about you.	What? Oh, of course, that project. Did you finish it?

Reinforce good behaviour, not bad. It's important to zero in on the behaviour you want not the behaviour you don't. This has the effect of reinforcing, or encouraging the repetition of, good behaviour while ignoring the bad. People hear what you say, not what you leave unsaid. And they usually want to be noticed and acknowledged. If children only and ever get attention when you tell them off, however unpleasant the process of being told off is, it's better than no attention at all. So when you pick up on the things you don't want and repeat them, instead of putting them off you actually encourage them to continue.

Insight

When you tell a child 'Don't ever put beans up your nose!' all the child hears is 'Beans', 'Up' and 'Nose'! However assertive you may be, being assertive over all the things you don't want can backfire on you.

Modelling what you want and being clear about what you would like pays off. Pay attention when they do something that pleases you and thank them for it rather than waiting for something that upsets you and drawing attention to it. Say what you want not what you don't want.

12 tips that can help you be more assertive:

1   *If you're negotiating or talking with someone and you want it to be amicable and the end result to be agreement, meet eye to eye and on the same level. If the other person is sitting down, sit down too; if they are standing, stand with them. If it's a child, go down to their eye-line. Being on the same level is disarming and comfortable and makes for equitable results.*

2   *If you're making a complaint or needing to assert yourself and take command, recognize that unequal levels can put you at an advantage. Standing over someone can put you in a dominant position, as can sitting behind a desk while they stand. You may need to take advantage of that, or be aware of how someone else is trying to do so to you.*

3   *Consider your body language. Crossed arms and crossed legs show you are defensive – make an effort to 'open up' by uncrossing and you'll send out confident vibes, which will make you feel more in control.*

4   *Being face to face can feel confrontational, being side by side can result in one of you being evasive or distracted. If it's discussion and negotiation you want, place yourself at a slight angle. If sitting, if necessary, move the chair to achieve this. If you need to assert yourself, look head on and make eye contact.*

5   *Watch your tone of voice. Keep it low, in volume and pitch. High pitch shows nervousness, loud voices*

are aggressive. If the person you're speaking to has to keep asking you to speak up, that puts you at a disadvantage. But if they have to make more effort to hear you that's a plus – they'll be paying attention to what you are saying.

6 *Have a plan – know what you want to achieve here, whether it's to have a pleasant chat with a family member or friend, to discuss something important with them, to get an agreement with someone at work, or to have your complaint heard. If you are not clear, suggest you postpone to another time.*

7 *Monitor your feelings, and those of the other person. If you realize either of you is beginning to feel angry, is sliding into acting aggressively or becoming unhappy, call a time out and suggest you continue when both of you are feeling better.*

8 *Accept you have the right to say no.*

9 *Look for models. Do you have assertive friends, colleagues, acquaintances? How do they do it? What do you feel about them? What can you take from their example?*

10 *Recognize it doesn't happen overnight. It might have taken you 20 years to have your confidence knocked out of you and to learn how NOT to be assertive. It's going to take less time to learn the skills of assertiveness, but it will take time. You'll do it a small step at a time. As the Chinese philosopher Lao-tzu said, 'A journey of a thousand miles begins with a single step.'*

11 *Celebrate every little triumph. Small ones, big ones – each brings you nearer the day when you won't bother to celebrate because it will be 'business as usual'.*

12 *Enjoy the process. Sometimes we focus so much on goals – the end of the journey – that we forget to take pleasure in getting there. You're learning new skills and making a difference day by day. Have fun as you do it!*

ASSERTIVENESS WITH PARENTS

One area in which many people find it difficult to be assertive is with their own parents. Parents knew you when you were a baby, a toddler, a child and a teenager. They watch you grow up and leave home but for many of them, that separation during the teenage years and that departure is hard to accept. It's as if they still see you as you were many years before – a child, needing their support and unable to cope on your own. When parents offer advice or help, it often grates. Sometimes this is because of how they do it and why they do it – as if they were still the adults and you the child. But sometimes, advice and suggestions you'd happily accept from a friend drive you into a rage when they come from a parent. It's not their manner or expectation which is at fault but your sensitivity to where it comes from.

You shouldn't have to tolerate behaviour from a relative that you wouldn't tolerate from a colleague, a friend or acquaintance. However, family are your support network; sometimes you have to accept that their behaviour may be undesirable and they may not see any reason to change. You can't change other people, you can only change yourself. But behaving differently yourself can have some powerful effects.

When parents visit or we go home to see them – at family festivals or at weekends – it's easy to fall back into familiar patterns of behaviour, with them and with siblings. Parents may treat their children as if they were, or should be, living at home again, to the bafflement and often fury of their partners. There may be criticism of the state of clothes, of whether you're eating enough or doing well enough, or of your children. Or parents may tell stories or conduct conversations in ways that say 'We were here first and this is where you have your primary loyalty' and that exclude the new people in their adult children's lives.

You may also find that when you see siblings, you all drop back into feeling, and behaving, they way you did when you were young and at home. Grown men and women may squabble, argue and fight over petty things. What you're actually doing is reviving quarrels from years ago – fighting over who gets the most attention, who are favourites, who comes first in your parents' eyes.

Preparing ahead
Being assertive on family visits requires some preparation. If you find them hard, ask yourself these questions:

▶ *What triggers set me off?*
▶ *What does it remind me of?*
▶ *How do I feel when I find it difficult?*

What triggers set me off?
Is it a tone of voice, a way of speaking to you, those family stories retold and retold? Sit down and think about the last time you were with them and put your finger on exactly what it was that upset you. Write them down.

What does it remind me of?
Then ask yourself – where does that particular behaviour take you? Does it remind you generally of being a child again or of specific incidents? What's the hook – how does it pull you back to the past? List these, too.

How do I feel when I find it difficult?
And most important of all, when you've answered the previous two questions, explore how it makes you feel. Angry? Jealous? Humiliated? Obligated? Under pressure to fulfil certain expectations? Do you feel you've been a disappointment or that you now have to come up to certain standards?

Once you can analyse what happens and why, you can plan in advance. Don't forget that when people seem to have power over you, it's only because you hand the power to them. You can claim it back. Seeing triggers and anticipating them means when they pop up, you can say 'Oh yes – the old family story which tells me I'm four years old again.' Forewarned is forearmed. These things have so much power because they operate under the level of conscious thought. Once you've brought them out into the open they lose much of their force. Once you know this behaviour hooks you back into feelings that properly belong in your past, you can pack them off there rather than allowing them to replay again. You can say 'Oh yes, I used to feel really angry/jealous/humiliated. But that was then. Now is now.'

Using your support network

It helps to discuss this with your support network – the people with whom you now have your first allegiance. It was right and proper that parents and siblings came first when you were a child and teenager. They were the centre of your world and what they thought of you, what they asked of you, should come first. As you moved through your teenage years you pulled away and friends became more and more important. It is right and natural during this period that friends' opinions matter more and more, but that family still play a large part in your life. But once you leave home, while family are your safety net, you should be shifting your focus on to your own life and needs, and a new support network – friends, and the family you begin on your own. If you have a partner, if you have children, they are your primary focus. Once you can see this, once they too can affirm that your unit comes first in your life, you can start to use the assertiveness techniques and strategies you are learning in this arena too.

Using 'I' statements, modelling what you want, using broken record, watching tone of voice and body language, prioritizing, giving feedback – all are as legitimate to use in your family as they are anywhere else. And you'd be surprised how effective they can be – and how quickly. And how much pleasanter than fighting the same battle again and again. You may also need to add one further strategy, which is to know when to refuse to be drawn, and to put that into action.

REFUSING TO BE INVOLVED

Sometimes your family, colleagues, friends or acquaintances have issues and want to involve you. It might be an argument between two siblings, two neighbours, two workmates, two friends and they appeal to you to be on their side. Maybe they feel they will have weight of numbers if they have you, or that you will bear out their argument if you agree with it. Often, when put in that situation we get hooked in; we worry and stress over which one to support. The trick is to recognize that you don't have to support either – to say 'I can't contribute so I'm bowing out' or 'I'm not going to be drawn into this, thank you.' When it comes to dealing with brothers or sisters still angry over something that happened years ago, why not try 'I know we used to fight like this when we were children. Now we're grown up, I'd far rather start again as adult friends.'

ASSERTIVENESS WITH IN-LAWS

Similarly, using assertiveness with in-laws can also make life a lot easier. Having an in-law treat your spouse as a child and their property, and you as an interloper, can make life really hard. The main difficulty here is that your partner needs to act too to really make changes. You can offer to sit down and go through the exercise outlined above and support each other in understanding what is going on and working together to do it differently. But even if they are not ready to make that step, you can do it for yourself. As we'll discuss in a later chapter, you can help other people to become assertive by modelling it for them in the way you now behave.

> ### Essential points to consider
>
> 1 *It is not a straight choice between either being liked or being assertive. Remember, no one likes a perpetual 'Yes' person or the doormat type. Real liking also means having real respect for someone.*
> 2 *You just have to accept sometimes that nothing you can do will ever really change someone. Then, it's time to move on.*
>
> *(Contd)*

3   Sometimes simply walking away from something you find offensive can send just as powerful a message and be more effective than joining in unresolvable arguments.

4   Giving and receiving constructive feedback is a good way to balance an argument and reach a good conclusion to it.

5   Pick your arena, think out what makes you feel good and therefore comfortable and then put your new-found assertiveness techniques into practice.

6   Reinforce good behaviour in others, not bad. Zero in on the behaviour you want, not on the behaviour you don't.

Insight

If you get in a panic, not knowing where to begin, close your eyes and picture how it might be if the situation were the way you would like it to be. Imagine it. Once you can see the situation as you would like, identify what elements are different to the way it is now. That gives you your action plan for what needs to change and then you can put it into action.

10 THINGS TO REMEMBER

1   *Being assertive is a skill you need to learn, not an art form you are born knowing.*

2   *Recognize that becoming assertive will take time. Unlearning some of the lessons that have made you what you are now will not happen overnight.*

3   *Being assertive is standing up for and by what you feel, think and mean.*

4   *Our physical presence – face, body language and speech – sets the scene for our emotional state. It should tell people we feel self-confident and have self-esteem and a sense of self-worth.*

5   *In relearning how to talk to show your new assertiveness, listen to how people you like, trust or respect do it and pick up tips.*

6   *Practice does make perfect. Practise your new skills – by yourself, in front of a mirror or with a sympathetic friend or family member. Use anything and everything that can help you reach your goal.*

7   *Never doubt that if anyone is trying to bully or dominate you, they are the one with the problem, not you.*

8   *Have reasonable, and attainable, expectations at every stage of your journey. You cannot become totally confident overnight and having unrealistic expectations can give you a false sense of failure.*

9   *One way to keep you going on your little-by-little progress to confidence and assertiveness is to give yourself a token reward for every gain you make.*

10 *Giving and receiving feedback can help you in becoming assertive.*

ASSERTIVENESS SCENARIOS

Assertiveness takes practice. Try these scenarios as examples with which to practise assertiveness skills. Respond assertively to each situation.

1   *A colleague of yours, whom you like, has a habit of wandering over to talk while you are working. You want to join in but would prefer to wait for a coffee break. It's 10 am, coffee is in half an hour and they arrive beside you – what do you say?*

2   *Your car has just been serviced, you've paid and as soon as you drive away you realize something you asked them to fix is still giving trouble. You turn around and go back – what do you say?*

3   *You paid a deposit to a builder to put a carport in your drive. The builder put up the frame but it still needs roofing. You haven't seen him for weeks – he's obviously gone off to do other work. He'd agreed to finish the job three months ago. You know of three other builders in your area wanting work – what do you say?*

4   *You come home after a long day to find the kitchen and bathroom in a mess – dirty dishes, dropped towels – and your partner in the living room watching TV, your children playing – what do you say?*

7

Accepting and giving criticism

In this chapter you will learn:
- *why criticism is hard to accept*
- *how to receive and how to give criticism*
- *how to deal with put-downs*
- *how to use the 'fogging' technique*
- *how to learn from your mistakes.*

Knowing how to both accept and give criticism in a positive way is key to being assertive. It sometimes seems as if we're surrounded by criticism – 'everyone's a critic', as they say. The fear of criticism is what puts many people off seeking to assert themselves. Nobody likes being held up and torn down unfairly. But we sometimes fear and avoid what can be seen as fair criticism even more. It's the anxiety about putting ourselves in the firing line and both attracting and having to deal with rigorous examination that can make us hold back.

So why do we all find criticism hard to accept? How can we take valid criticism on board and how do we deal with it? What should we do when judgements are being made and we don't feel they are valid? And how should we ourselves deliver criticism so it is helpful?

Dealing with criticism

Whenever criticism is offered, the questions you might like to ask yourself are:

▶ *Is this intended to encourage and support or undermine?*
▶ *Is this helpful – will it encourage and support or undermine?*
▶ *How can I now go forward with this criticism?*

WAS THE CRITICISM INTENDED TO ENCOURAGE AND SUPPORT OR UNDERMINE?

The motives of the person offering it, and their actual intention, can be significant. However, whether criticism helps or not isn't always about whether it was intended as a help or a hindrance. It depends on the attitude of the person on the receiving end, and what they take from it. Someone can give you a positive, thoughtful assessment with the very best intentions and if you are feeling defensive it can simply feel like an attack. On the other hand, someone can be judgmental and disparaging with the main intention of hurting your feelings, and if you are self-confident and know your worth, you can actually take something from it.

When receiving criticism, it's worthwhile taking a moment to work out the probable intention of the critic. This can help you because sometimes you need to dive under their words or behaviour. If you can determine they wanted to undermine you rather than help you, you may need to choose to sidestep what has been said. Being assertive often means knowing when you don't have to take on board something that has been offered to you.

Insight

Unfair, destructive judgements that really have as a main aim an intention to undermine you can be rejected. It's a bit like being offered a parcel. Just because it's been handed to you doesn't mean you have to take it, unwrap it and accept the contents. Sometimes you have to say 'Sorry – not mine. I'll just leave this here or hand it back, thanks.'

But even if the intention was hurtful, you still may recover something useful from what is being said. You could take much of what is offered with some scepticism, but there may be some truth in it and that might be useful.

Listen even if you don't like what you hear
Criticism offered with the intention of being helpful should always be considered, even if you don't like what you hear. You may still decide to reject what is being said, but at least it's important to think about what is being offered. Friends, family or colleagues who take the risk of being shot as the messenger by telling you something unwelcome may well have a message you need to listen to.

When offering criticism, consider why you are giving it. Are you upset or angry, and wanting to make that plain? Do you want to cut the person down to size? Do you want to make yourself or your achievements look better by giving them doubts or reducing theirs? Or is your motive to help them do better, to boost their confidence and their abilities? Sometimes the painful truth is that we have destructive and negative reasons for offering what we do, and we need to consider and examine these before saying anything. If you're angry or upset, it's better to say so rather than using roundabout ways of delivering a reproof. It doesn't get to the heart of the problem if you hand out a stinging attack on someone's work or their leaving the bathroom in a mess, when what is really bothering you is that they didn't consult you, or are taking you for granted – or haven't said they love you in a week! And it won't help if you attack them personally rather than focusing on what it is they did to upset you.

IS THIS CRITICISM HELPFUL – WILL IT ENCOURAGE AND SUPPORT OR UNDERMINE?

Even destructive criticism that is meant to undermine can be turned to an advantage. You need, however, to ask yourself this question because what often at first seems hurtful and difficult is actually intended to help. A significant aspect to look at is whether it's your behaviour that is being held up for examination, or you. Helpful criticism always highlights behaviour, not people. When someone says, for instance, 'You're lazy', 'You're nasty' or 'You're selfish', it is personal – the individual is being attacked, and labelled. When you're told 'You are....', where can you go? It's hard to move forward when you're stuck with being whatever it is that has upset the person saying this. When, instead, what is pointed to is a particular bit of behaviour – and the more specific the better – we can address that. So, instead of 'You're lazy', what might be said is 'I asked you to take out the rubbish and you didn't – please do it now.' Instead of 'You're nasty', what might be said is 'When you said that you hurt my feelings.' Instead of 'You're selfish', what might be said is 'It upset me that you made that arrangement without consulting with me first.' When we address the behaviour rather than the person, we begin to move towards a solution.

Insight

What you and anyone you deal with would benefit from is mutual respect, and that comes when people only give fair analysis, not criticism as a method of getting their own way.

Think about what you say and how you say it. Don't forget, your words only tell a fraction of the story. Whether you make eye contact, your stance, the tone and level of your voice all contribute to making both giving and receiving criticism a positive experience.

| Positive | | Negative | |
| Assertive | | Non-assertive | |
Body language	What it means	Body language	What it means
Eye contact	You mean what you say, have good intentions and you want to communicate	Looking away	You have no confidence, may not have good intentions and are avoiding listening or taking another viewpoint on board
Leaning forward	You are listening	Leaning back	You are defensive and not listening
Arms loose	You are open and receptive	Arms crossed	You are defensive and may be hostile
Low voice	You are confident	High, loud voice	You are nervous

HOW CAN I NOW GO FORWARD WITH THIS CRITICISM?

In some – possibly, many – cases, criticism is valid: they're right. How do you react assertively to criticism? You accept it. But you do so cheerfully, with a desire to do better in the future, and no intention of letting it make you feel bad about yourself or blame yourself. You don't take it personally, even if there was a personal element.

So if a friend or work colleague complains you're late arriving, say 'Yes, you're right. I need to organize my time better.' Don't make excuses and certainly don't lie to cover yourself. Even if you feel it wasn't your fault – a late train, someone at home distracting you – still take the responsibility. After all, the chances are with more thought or foresight you could have been on time. So own it, and change your behaviour if you want to, or don't change if you don't want to – but either way, don't beat yourself up or let it lead to an argument just because you've been criticized.

Another way of taking responsibility is simply owning up to your mistakes before anyone says anything. Again, you turn up late and the first thing you say is 'I'm late – sorry! My fault and I will do better from now on.' By acknowledging the problem and accepting responsibility for the situation, you take back control.

Dealing positively with criticism

Dealing positively with criticism requires you to listen, acknowledge, assess and come up with answers. If what has been said feels difficult and painful to take on board, ask for a time to assess the situation – to cool down and collect your thoughts. Don't let yourself be hustled into reacting immediately if you need this time. You're not using it to look for a defence or a way out of the situation – you're looking for a way of managing what has been said in the best possible manner.

If an immediate reply is demanded, a useful thing to say is 'It's a no if you want an answer at once; a probable yes if you can give me some time to think.'

Often if you're struggling with criticism it helps to ask for elaboration or rephrasing. If criticism is given indirectly, ask for a direct statement. You can't deal head on with games-playing, you can with honesty. Opening up the situation may help you see a solution. The more specific it is, the better for all of you. You, to see what you might be able to do to improve things. Them, to perhaps see what they saw as a problem isn't quite as bad as they thought. And for both of you, to focus your minds on moving on rather than being stuck. The most important tip for handling criticism is to accept responsibility. That might mean accepting you made a mistake or it might mean your carrying the buck for someone else, because the ultimate accountability was yours. Whatever, sometimes that is all you can do and all that is required.

Of course, if you don't agree, or partially agree, say so and why. This is why asking for the criticism to be specific is so important. Simply saying 'I don't agree' can sound defensive and inauthentic. You're simply refusing to examine what has been said or to entertain the sentiments being offered. But if you have been told 'You did such and such' or 'You failed to do so and so' and you can give specific examples to contradict, or to modify what has been suggested, you can show that you are willing to change if change is what is required.

Case study

Lee was struggling to get on with his teenage son, who he felt defied him at every turn and went out of his way to oppose him. Lee reluctantly went with his wife Tonia to a series of parenting discussions at his son's school. Once there he was surprised to find himself among so many other parents also worrying about their children's behaviour – Lee had felt he was the only one among his friends to be having such difficulties and his unwillingness to go had been because he did not want to be shown up. Once he realized he was not alone, he found it easier to think about what was going on between him and his son. Lee recalled his own father, who had been formal and authoritarian, and very critical of Lee. Lee realized he fell automatically into a similar pattern and that he saw in his son an enthusiasm and boisterousness he wished he had been able to express. He was jealous. Once he could see that, Lee began to practise being positive and forthcoming to his son, and stopped criticizing him. Not only was he delighted at the way their relationship improved, he was astonished to find his son also stopped opposing him.

Essential points to consider

1   *Being able to accept and give fair criticism is one of the keys to being assertive.*
2   *Establishing what kind of criticism – valid or not, supportive or undermining – will help you deal with it better. So will working out the probable intentions of your critic.*
3   *When it is you that is the critic, consider honestly the reasons why you are doing it before you offer your criticism.*

Dealing with put-downs

How do you manage when you realize the other person isn't so much criticizing you as putting you down and when the sole motive for their remarks appears to be to depress and upset you and to take control of the situation? When someone puts you down, a natural response is to want to get your own back or to defend yourself. Defending yourself usually has a negative impact on both you and the other person. This often escalates into conflict – arguments, backbiting and feuds.

Put-downs hook you into feeling insecure and low in self-worth. But they're really about the insecurity and low self-worth of the person doing it to you. They're relying on you responding in a way that boosts their ego and sense of power and control. When you react, especially by going on the defensive, you do just that. Put-downs rely on a reaction from you.

When dealing with a put-down you can:

▶ *Ignore it. This is about others trying to make themselves feel better at your expense. You don't owe them the duty of making them feel better by your feeling worse. So let the remark float over your head. They're likely to stop when you do not give them the satisfaction of a reaction.*
▶ *Laugh at it. Don't deal with the remark full-on but make a joke that deflects and defuses the situation.*
▶ *Address the underlying need – that of the other person's need to feel better. Ask them if there is anything with which you can help, encourage and support them. Suggest that since there seems to be a problem perhaps co-operation between the two of you might solve it.*

Fogging

One technique that often proves useful when faced with unfair criticism, or criticism that has a main aim of getting at you, is fogging. Fogging is a strategy that can defuse the power of criticism to hurt or depress you. It's a helpful approach when what you're being offered is negative and unfair. Fogging is so named because instead of going head to head in conflict, you offer no apparent resistance. If you stand your ground someone can attack you. If you turn and run, they can pursue you. But if you imagine a bank of fog blowing up and enveloping both of you, you can see your critic can get lost. And when you're lost in a fog, there's no point fighting it or shouting at it; it simply melts away and so resists your attempts at intimidation or influence. What you do with fogging is to agree, deflect, and remain calm and reasonable. You do not allow yourself to be provoked or upset by what is being said. You consider what is said, agree with whatever may be fair and useful and turn the criticism around. Fogging requires some self-control, but it can be enormously effective.

So, for instance, if your teenager turns up their nose at your spaghetti bolognaise, saying 'Yuck, I'm not eating that, it's horrible!', you could be hurt by the criticism or angry at the rejection. Or, you could recognize that all teenagers have to rebel and needle their parents and you might say 'Oh, I am sorry you don't like it. There's bread in the bin, and I'm sure we can share yours out between us or maybe the cat would like it...'

Or if a family member or work colleague takes exception to what you have done and becomes abusive, rather than being crushed by the name-calling or tempted to answer back, tackle it at face value. 'Stupid? Well, I suppose we can all behave stupidly at times. Compared to Einstein I'm no genius...'

The point of fogging is that it robs your critic's words of their destructive power. You may find it hard at first because it feels as if you're backing down and giving in. But your refusal to become upset or angry in the face of criticism is the strongest defence of all. By remaining calm, you're denying your critic the satisfaction of seeing you upset or browbeaten and of losing control and having your power taken away. If what is at the root of their behaviour is an attempt to bully you, and it doesn't succeed, your critic is likely to back off. Like that fog, you just melt away before them, leaving them hitting out at the mist.

Useful phrases to use when fogging are: 'That could be true', 'I see what you mean', 'I'm sorry you feel that way', 'You may be right' and 'You have a point there.' What you hold firm to while fogging is the recognition that whatever the criticism, justified or not, you will learn from what is being said but you will not give up your power or control or your good self-image of yourself.

Essential points to consider

1   *When offering or receiving criticism, how you say things – your body language, your tone and expression – is just as important as what you say.*
2   *A put-down is usually more about the needs of the person doing it than it is about the one being criticized.*
3   *The 'fogging' technique is often the best strategy for dealing with unfair criticism or a put-down.*

Learning from your mistakes

An important aspect of assertiveness is the ability to learn from mistakes, and then move on. When we're being passive, passive-aggressive or aggressive we dwell, deny or nag about these. We criticize others unfairly, trying to shift responsibility or blame, and we go into avoidance when someone criticizes us. You dwell and obsess about the smallest issue, when you can't set it aside. The trick is to accept and encompass, learn and then move forward. You can't be perfect; everyone makes mistakes and that's OK. Accepting that fact is really important because when you believe that perfection exists and you have to aspire to it, you can find yourself in trouble. You may stop trying and fall back, despondent and believing you can never achieve anything. You may close your ears to anything anyone says, refusing valid criticism in an effort to escape what you see as painful slights. Refusing to learn or refusing to try are equally unhelpful. Or you become particularly and unrealistically critical of others, demanding standards that no one can achieve. Assertiveness demands that you go on pushing boundaries and taking risks, even if it leads to your making more mistakes, but accepting that perfection is a snare and a delusion.

Insight

According to the World Database of Happiness, Iceland, in spite of being bankrupt, dark and cold, is the happiest place on earth. One reason may be that Icelanders do not have a culture of perfection. Which may be why they have more artists per capita than any nation; people are willing to give it a go.

10 THINGS TO REMEMBER

1 *Knowing how to accept and to give criticism positively is a key to being assertive.*

2 *Fear of criticism can be a major holdback to becoming assertive.*

3 *Learn to distinguish what sort of criticism you are facing – is it there to encourage and support, or to undermine or put down?*

4 *When you are offering criticism, always consider why you are giving it.*

5 *When receiving criticism, dive under the words to assess the probable intention of the critic before you react to it.*

6 *Like bullying, the put-down relies on getting a reaction from you. Look for and address the underlying need – what is the other person's real problem that makes them do this to you?*

7 *Where appropriate, use the 'fogging' technique to deal with unfair criticism.*

8 *Recognize that you need self-worth, self-esteem and confidence more than another person's approval.*

9 *Learn from your mistakes and then move on, don't dwell on them.*

10 *Being assertive means you have to take occasional risks, even if it leads to your making more mistakes.*

QUIZ

1 *Which do you find more difficult?*
   a *fair criticism*
   b *unfair criticism.*

2 *When someone criticizes what's your immediate reaction? To:*
   a *explain what went wrong*
   b *listen to what is being said.*

3 *When you criticize do you do it:*
   a *to help the person do it differently next time*
   b *make them see what they did wrong.*

4 *When giving or receiving criticism are you likely to:*
   a *lean forwards and make eye contact*
   b *have your arms crossed and speak loudly.*

5 *The last time you were critical, did you:*
   a *tell the other person exactly what they had done*
   b *tell them they had been lazy or messy or something similar.*

6 *The last time someone was critical to you, did you feel:*
   a *the criticism was about something you had done*
   b *the criticism was about something in their life.*

How did you do?

1a: Your anxiety is about putting yourself to the test. You need to acknowledge that fair criticism is an opportunity to help you change and do better.

1b: Unfair criticism is annoying and upsetting, but it tells you more about the person making it than you. You still need to hear what is being said in case it contains something that can be of use to you, but you shouldn't let it hurt you.

2a: It's tempting to argue and make excuses but all this does is stop you listening to what has been said, which may well be useful. Next time, bite your lip, hear what is being said and accept it as an opportunity.

2b: Whether the criticism was fair or unfair, it's wise to listen and take something from it.

3a: You're offering fair criticism in a fair way – very assertive!

3b: You need to go back and read this chapter again. It's far more efficient and assertive to have as your main motive the desire to help, not to score points.

4a: You've taken on board the need to be open and connected to anyone when giving or receiving criticism.

4b: Unassertive body language can undermine the help you might be offering. Go back and read again about using non-verbal ways of getting your message across.

5a: Being specific is helpful when delivering fair criticism. It tells the other person exactly what they need to work on.

5b: Labelling people – saying they are lazy instead of telling them what you'd expected them to do – means they have nowhere to go. Go back and look again at more effective ways of getting the message across.

6a: Criticism, whether fair or unfair, about your own actions should always be considered, assessed and used to improve yourself.

6b: If you feel the criticism was really about where your critic was in life rather than what you did, 'fog' or sidestep it, or offer support and help to the person making it.

8

Accepting and giving compliments

In this chapter you will learn:
- *to value yourself*
- *to value other people*
- *the importance of giving and receiving compliments*
- *how to accept and give compliments*
- *how to use a 'Self-Worth Wall'.*

You probably agree that accepting and giving criticism would be a difficult issue for most of us. We fear being judged and often do our utmost to avoid it. How we deal with criticism is clearly an important part of learning to be assertive, and it's easy to realize that. What we may not recognize is that how we deal with compliments, both the accepting and the giving of them, is actually equally important and significant.

Valuing ourselves and others

Giving and accepting compliments is vital to being assertive for one important reason: they relate to how we value ourselves, and how we value others. Value is an important concept when dealing with assertiveness. We can assert ourselves when we recognize our own value – that we are worthwhile, that we deserve to be respected and that we respect ourselves, and those around us. And indeed, we can allow other people to be assertive without reverting to being passive, passive-aggressive or aggressive with them when we can recognize their value too, and see it as complementary to ours, not in competition. Not having been valued in childhood is often the reason why people are unassertive and have low self-esteem and low self-confidence. Part of learning to assert ourselves is learning also to value ourselves.

So how we accept and give compliments is as relevant to assertiveness as is accepting and giving criticism. And how do we generally deal with compliments? In our culture, on the whole, badly!

Think of the last time someone paid you a compliment. Did you:

▶ *refuse it*
▶ *trivialize it*
▶ *undermine it.*

Refuse it. When someone compliments us, we often push them away, snubbing them and insisting that we don't want to accept what they say. We laugh, flap our hands and say something along the lines of 'Please don't make a fuss!'

Trivialize it. Compliments are often met with a denial. When, for instance, someone remarks on what an attractive outfit you are wearing, you may respond 'What, this old thing?'

Undermine it. When someone remarks on what a good job you have done, it's frequently met with 'Oh no, it was nothing, really.'

What is the result of not accepting compliments?

We refuse, trivialize or undermine compliments for several reasons. It might be because:

We're embarrassed. If we're struggling with issues of self-esteem and confidence, we may not like to be in the spotlight. Accepting a compliment may feel like making yourself vulnerable – and putting yourself in the position of having to come up with the goods again!

We feel we don't deserve them. Lacking the self-esteem to accept you deserve a compliment may be the most important reason we refuse them.

We feel we should be modest. Decades of being told 'Don't be boastful', 'Don't get above yourself' or 'You're no one special' often leaves us with the conviction that we shouldn't seek or accept compliments, because doing so is bad manners.

BUT HOW DOES OUR REFUSAL STRIKE OTHER PEOPLE?

Perhaps the last generation, or the one before that, appreciates such conduct. But the reality is that when you give a compliment and it is refused, trivialized or undermined, you don't admire this behaviour. Instead, you feel:

Rebuffed. You offered a gift or what you knew was earned and had it thrown back in your face.

Insulted. You made a judgment and expressed it, and had the other person in effect tell you your judgement was wrong.

Unimpressed. Instead of feeling the person refusing the compliment was being appropriately modest, we're more likely to think they were being inappropriately self-effacing.

Case study

Bea and Joe came for counselling, and Bea said from the beginning she was only coming to help Joe accept the fact that she had decided their relationship was over. Joe seemed resigned to her going but said he just wanted to understand it. Eventually she told him the final straw had been when he turned down a promotion at work because he felt he wouldn't manage the new job, which Bea said he could do
(Contd)

standing on his head. 'I can't do that,' he protested, 'It's right outside my level!' 'There you go,' she said 'that's why I decided to leave. When I congratulated him on running a half marathon I got the usual "Oh, I was cr*p, it was my worst time, everyone else I know did it faster, I'll never be any good at this." And now this. I'm fed up of it. Any time I say something nice to the man, he tells me I don't know what I'm talking about. I can't live with this anymore.'

HOW TO ACCEPT A COMPLIMENT

An important aspect of assertiveness is acknowledging and accepting compliments. Doing so means you appreciate what other people think of you and hear their views on your abilities, skills and choices. It isn't being arrogant or selfish, nor does it mean you take anything away from anyone else to gracefully say 'Thank you!' when someone says 'Well done' or 'I like that'. Phrases you might find helpful are:

'Thank you!'
'I'm glad you like it.'
'I'm pleased you enjoyed it.'
'I appreciate your saying that.'
'That's very kind of you.'
If you feel other people contributed you can also say:
'I'll pass on your compliment to the rest of them.'
'I'm sure everyone will be glad to hear that.'

When accepting compliments, don't let your body language or tone undercut what you are saying. Make eye contact, smile and use open gestures to reinforce your message that you hear what is being said, accept it and acknowledge it.

Insight

Somebody recently told me I was always cheerful, always positive, always confident, and thus always inspirational. I was initially surprised – was that really how I came across? And then I shook myself. Of course that was how I came across – it was how I worked to come across. So I thanked her. I told her I really appreciated hearing that. I didn't

always feel as positive, confident and cheerful as perhaps
I seemed but it was really good to know that I was projecting
surety if the result was reassuring or inspiring to others.

Most importantly, take the compliment away, think about and use
it. If self-esteem, self-worth and self-confidence are issues for you,
compliments are part of your toolbox to raise them. One thing you
should have in your home is a Self-Worth Wall.

The Self-Worth Wall

Every home should have one. Choose somewhere in your home
that you see every day. It could be in the hallway or in the kitchen.
Use the whole wall, or put up a notice board. This is where
you and anyone else in your home is going to blow their own
trumpet. Make a note of any and all achievements. You could
stick up certificates or letters, or emails. When someone pays you
a compliment face to face or on the phone or by text, make a note
of it and pin it here, so you can see it and be reminded of it, and
so can everyone else. 'John told me I did a really good job of that
project today!', 'Sarah said I looked especially nice in my new
dress.' Encourage your whole family to do this for themselves;
it's a good idea for all of you to add little notes and anything
else that catches your fancy to pass on a message of support and
appreciation.

Insight

A family I know buy each other fridge magnets. When they
want to say 'Well done!' or 'I was thinking of you' they pick
out a magnet they know that particular person will like (mum
is into food themes, the youngest loves cats) and put it on the
fridge door with a note saying 'This is for you because...'

You do need to raise your self-esteem and self-confidence, and
increase your appreciation of your own worth in order to be
assertive. Which is why, as well as being able to recognize and
accept compliments, you need to understand that the person you

most need to approve of you is yourself. You are the ultimate judge of your own behaviour. When you see that and can respect yourself, other people's compliments become a pleasure to hear. But they are not what you need to chase after or seek. You know what you deserve and are worth already. Being reliant on what other people think of you is the enemy of assertiveness. It's nice and it's pleasant to hear what they say and know what they think. But it's not the be-all and end-all.

> ### Insight
> Needing outside approval makes you needy and desperate, and prone to doing what will achieve someone else's approval rather than what is right or right for you.

How should you raise your own self-esteem? The Self-Worth Wall is an excellent strategy. What would work in your life?

Give a stroke, receive a stroke

A 'stroke' is any action that tells someone you're happy to see them, pleased to be with them and glad about something they might have done. Strokes may be verbal, when you say 'Thank you' or 'I liked that'. They can also be actions, such as making someone a cup of coffee or giving them a hug. When we give strokes it 'models' behaviour – lets people see how nice it is and how to do it. Give strokes and you soon find them coming back at you. We can, and should, also give ourselves strokes – help yourself to an apple, settle down with a magazine, book or TV programme knowing it's right and proper and deserved that you have this time to yourself, doing what you want.

> ### Insight
> What did you do today that pleased you? Look for moments that you can identify as being worthy of some self-congratulation. It can be as simple as doing the ironing, making a phone call you were putting off, taking out the rubbish. If it took some effort and you made it: well done.

Reward yourself, regularly. You make small gains and small victories all the time and the more you recognize that, the higher your esteem will be – and the better you will perform. Pats on the back from other people are welcome but one from yourself is actually just as, if not more, valuable. Rewards can be small – a glass of wine with dinner, a few moments online emailing friends – or large – deciding you will go on that special holiday you've always dreamed about this year. But the act of rewarding yourself – of recognizing you deserve a treat because you deserve recognition – is the key thing.

Insight

Whenever I hear that someone I know has done something praiseworthy – perhaps one of my godsons has passed an exam – as well as offering my hearty congratulations, I always ask – are you pleased with yourself? If you only feel validated when in other people's eyes, you may have to wait a long time, and they may also miss the real achievements. Which isn't always in the winning but in the striving. You always know how well you deserved acclaim, and you should offer it to yourself because you should seek to gain your own approval before you seek that of others. It's really nice to be praised. It's even better to have that warm glow of satisfaction because you know you did well.

Giving compliments and the four Ss

The rule for giving compliments is to use the four Ss – Small, Simple, Spontaneous and Specific.

Small. What you say or how you recognize merit need not be elaborate or extensive. The fact of saying or doing it is more important than the reward. So, just saying 'Thanks!' or 'Bravo!' or offering a biscuit with that cup of coffee is sufficient to get over the message that you noticed and think they deserve a pat on the back. You should never hold back from giving small and frequent compliments and affirmations of people's worth and ability – that's nice, that's pretty, that was well done.

Simple. A single daffodil picked from your own garden when given with affection or respect – or both! – as a way of recognizing merit is worth any hand-tied bouquet if you mean it. You should never feel your offering is too simple or not elaborate enough.

Insight

One of my friends often arrives for lunch or dinner with a mixture of wild and cultivated flowers, herbs and shrubs cut from her garden. I love receiving bought bunches of flowers but somehow the fact that she has gone out and picked though her hedgerows and beds means a lot to me.

Spontaneous. Sometimes, measured and thought out praise has great worth, showing you've carefully considered what you want to say. But often there is no substitute for an instant reaction that says 'I just had to speak up at once!' People often bite their lip, feeling a compliment or comment would be out of place or inappropriate and by the time they realize it would be welcome, the moment feels as if it has passed. You should always speak up or act with that touch on the arm or hug when it strikes you.

Specific. Saying 'Well done!' or 'Bravo' or 'You did fine!' can sometimes be helpful, but being specific can be the best way of raising self-esteem. General praise can give a warm glow but often we're not sure exactly what it was for – what behaviour of ours the person passing the compliment actually appreciated. When you are specific, you tell the person exactly what it was you liked. Not only do they know where they stand with you, they also have every incentive to repeat it. 'You hung up the towels in the bathroom. Thank you!'; 'That casserole you made was delicious!'; 'You did that job on time, and did it well – bravo.'

Giving descriptive praise

Descriptive praise is an excellent strategy for giving specific compliments. When we're pleased with someone, we often tell them that they are 'good' or say 'well done'. This is great, but often it doesn't actually tell the person what they've done, why we like it and what we would like them to continue doing. It tells them about us, that *we* are happy, but it doesn't tell them about *them*, that they are capable and competent. Descriptive praise does exactly this. So, when you come home and find your teenager has washed up after having a snack and fed the cat, instead of 'Aren't you good!' say 'You fed the cat and washed up. You cleared the deck so now I can get on with preparing a meal. That was really helpful. Thank you!' Instead of thinking 'Yeah, well, whatever... but what did I do?' the teenager thinks 'Yeah! I'm really helpful! I can do that!' and has every incentive to repeat the behaviour, and a clear idea of what you appreciate. Giving descriptive praise sounds a bit odd at first – itemizing exactly what has been done feels so awkward. Start doing it and you'll soon realize how easy it is, and how very effective. 'You did all the washing up before I came home. Thank you!'; 'You stayed by me when we went to the supermarket and helped me fill the trolley. Thank you!'; 'You wrote that report and included all the elements we'd discussed. Thank you!'

10 THINGS TO REMEMBER

1 A large part of becoming assertive is learning how to value yourself and how to compliment yourself.

2 Learning how to handle compliments is just as important as knowing how to deal with criticism.

3 Don't be modest. It is not 'bad manners' or 'boastful', whatever you may have been taught, to recognize and accept an earned or justified compliment.

4 Don't refuse, trivialize or undermine any compliments received.

5 If you handle the receipt of a compliment badly, you will probably leave the giver feeling rebuffed, insulted or unimpressed.

6 When accepting a compliment make sure your body language matches what you are saying. Make eye contact, smile and use open gestures to reinforce your response.

7 Make use of the Self-Worth Wall, or any similar strategy, to encourage or praise yourself and those around you for things achieved or compliments received.

8 Reward yourself regularly in recognition of the fact that you make small gains and have small victories all the time.

9 The golden rule for giving compliments is the four Ss. Make them Small, Simple, Spontaneous and Specific.

10 Use descriptive praise when you can. Don't just say 'Good' or 'Well done' but tell the person you are complimenting what they have actually done to make you so pleased with them.

EXERCISE

Before you go on to the next chapter, you should:

1   *Create your Self-Worth Wall, and put your first piece of self-praise on it.*

2   *Make a list – at least three each – of the strokes you would like to give someone else, and the strokes you would like to receive. Give some of the former; tell or show another person about the ones you'd like.*

3   *Give a compliment using the four Ss – Small, Simple, Spontaneous and Specific.*

4   *Praise someone, using descriptive praise – telling them exactly what they did to please you.*

You may feel awkward doing one, some or all of these. Reread the relevant sections if needs be to have clear in your mind what you should do, how to do it, and why. Then swallow your anxiety and give it a go. Note how you feel afterwards, and the immediate effect it has. It may not register with the other person or they may try to shrug it off. Persist and you will find it has positive results.

9

Saying no

In this chapter you will learn:
- *how to say 'No' effectively*
- *why saying 'Yes' can land you in trouble*
- *that making excuses isn't effective*
- *about matching body language to what you say.*

One of the most difficult areas for most unassertive people is being able to say no. If you're struggling with being submissive or passive, the likelihood is that you say yes all the time – yes to helping people out, yes to taking on other people's responsibilities as your own, yes to doing far too much.

Insight

As an agony aunt, I'd say a large number of the appeals I receive are about not being able to say no. From the woman whose friend assumes she'll baby-sit, through the man who doesn't want to spend his nights getting drunk with his mates, to the couple who want a quiet wedding but have mothers who want a massive do. All find those three little words 'Thanks but no' so hard to say.

Saying no so it doesn't offend

If you find yourself reverting to aggressive or passive-aggressive modes when faced with calls on your time you may indeed be able to say no. But in doing so, you may alienate and upset people either by being abrupt or hostile, or by complaining and grumbling. The assertive option is to be able to refuse, but to do so leaving everyone feeling OK about it. That takes skill and practice.

Saying no is often felt to be selfish, callous and cruel. You may fear others will think you petty-minded or mean, aggressive or ill-mannered if you turn down a perfectly reasonable request to help them out. Most of us will lie, fudge or shift responsibility when faced with being asked to do something we don't want to do or that will cause us problems. Instead of saying 'No, I won't' we try to soften the blow by saying 'Oh, I can't':

'My cousin's coming to stay.'
'I'm washing my hair that night.'
'Oh, what a pity – we're already committed.'
'I'd love to, I really would but I think we're busy so I'll say yes and let you know tomorrow…'
'Oh, I'd have loved to come but my husband has already arranged something and he'll be furious if I change it…'

MAKING EXCUSES DOESN'T WORK

The problem with making excuses is that it doesn't tackle the real problem. It might postpone matters by getting you off the hook that particular time. But since in making an excuse you actually agree that they could call on you – the only reason you're not doing it on this occasion is because of the circumstances – all that happens is they come back again some other time. What you need to do is twofold: consider whether you should be saying yes or no in the first place, and learn some techniques for making your decision stick.

Women, parents and adult children have the hardest time saying no. Many people still believe the myth that when a woman says no she means yes. Women, particularly mothers, are expected to be the ones who put their own needs and time second to that of their partners or families, and our own parents still assume that if they ask we shouldn't say no. It's not only women – many men, in their personal lives and their work lives, also have a problems with saying 'No, shan't, don't want to!'

Of course we all have duties and obligations in our lives. What you need to remember is that it's only in your job that you might be expected to do as you are asked and told – and even then, only within your terms of contract. In many aspects of your working life and in all aspects of your private life what you have is a delicate balance of mutual help and responsibility. The vital element to keep in mind is that it's mutual. It should be 'I'll do this for you and you'll do that for me.' You need the ability to say no in situations where it tends to be all one way – you doing stuff for them but them doing nothing like as much for you. If you're the person who does all the cleaning and tidying up at home, or does all the ferrying around, because it seems easier than getting into an argument over it; who agrees to things you'd rather not do, or gets landed with work that isn't yours; who finds yourself late at the end of the day getting your own work done after you've finished everyone else's; who swallows your resentment when you are 'volunteered' for something you don't want to do; or who maybe trembles at the idea of having to be tougher with someone who defies you – you need to learn to say no.

WHY YOU SHOULD LEARN TO SAY NO

So where do you start? You begin by settling a few home truths in your own mind:

▶ *You have the right to say no.*
▶ *Just because someone asks, doesn't mean you have to do what they request.*
▶ *You're being neither rude nor unfair to refuse.*
▶ *If you never say no what is your yes worth?*
▶ *You'll respect and like yourself more if you stand up for yourself.*
▶ *Other people will respect and like you more if you stand up for yourself.*

You have the right to say no. Understanding that this is a right is the beginning. Of course there are times when people rely on you or need you. Naturally there are times when you would choose to do what is asked. But it's up to you and your judgement to know when. You can say no.

Just because someone asks, doesn't mean you have to do what they request. It's very easy to bow to someone's need. They want you, they ask for you and their urgency or sense of entitlement can sweep you up. But just because the request or demand has been made doesn't mean you have to give in to it.

You're being neither rude nor unfair to refuse. They have the right to ask and equally you have the right to refuse. Just because someone else wants you to do something doesn't mean they have priority or privilege. It just means they stepped forward. You can equally step back and it isn't a personal insult or failing in you when you do so.

If you never say no what is your yes worth? There is no sense of it being a special gift or a favour when the eternal yes person says yes. If you always say yes, others will take it for granted and hardly value it. But when your yes is something to be earned, it can be fully appreciated when given.

You'll respect and like yourself more if you stand up for yourself. You may try to persuade yourself that when you give in all the time you have a warm glow of satisfaction. You do so much for people! Doesn't that give you points? The reality is that being a doormat leads to frustration and resentment, and a lack of respect for yourself. Begin to stand up for yourself and you will find you feel far more positive about yourself.

Other people will respect and like you more if you stand up for yourself. Other people feel the same way. Nobody respects the eternal fall-guy, the person who runs themselves ragged trying to please everybody else. Once you begin to stand tall, other people will not only respect you more but like you more too. They may regret not having the constant help, but having to take more responsibility for themselves too spreads the message about self-confidence, self-esteem and self-worth.

Insight

If you can accept it when people say no to you, it's time you recognized you can do the same to them. If you don't, then it's time to look at your respect for others as well as your respect for yourself.

How should you say no?

So how do you do it?

Pre-empt if possible. If you know someone is bearing down on you, ready to ask a favour; if you know when the phone goes it's going to be that friend or relative, expecting you to drop everything for them, get in first. Say 'Before we go on, can I just say I'm really busy today and I'm not going to be able to help you out.' Be pleasant but firm. And use broken record if they insist. You can always say 'I'm going to have to interrupt you and go. Lovely to see/speak with you. Goodbye!'

You can give a simple 'No'. You don't owe them an explanation. You may give reasons but certainly not excuses. Unless you're in the Forces or another emergency occupation, you're not in a situation where someone in authority can tell you what to do and it's a sacking offence if you refuse. You don't need to carry an assumption of having to do something over into your private life. You might choose to add:

▶ *I would prefer not to, thank you.*
▶ *I'm not willing to, thank you*
▶ *I don't want to, thank you.*

If you might say yes but on your terms, check out the request and don't respond immediately. Ask for more information and clarification about what is wanted, when, where and for how long. In order to keep control of the situation you might like to say 'If you want an immediate answer it's no. If you give me time to think about it, it might be yes.'

Being direct and honest works. White lies, excuses or playing for time tend to end up in the worst of all worlds. You'll either have to work increasingly and desperately hard at avoiding what or whoever it was, and still end up doing it, or upset and alienate them and make yourself feel bad. If you are not direct, it can lead to several problems:

▶ *People continue to ask you to do things because you've not said 'No', only 'Not at the moment'.*
▶ *You feel resentful, angry and guilty.*
▶ *You have to keep track of your excuses and white lies.*
▶ *People begin to feel you are avoiding or stringing them along.*

On the other hand, a direct 'No' has many benefits:

▶ *It saves time – if you can't or don't want to do it, the request ends there.*
▶ *Everyone knows exactly where they stand.*
▶ *You can negotiate a better deal for you if you do choose to help – a win/win solution for everyone.*
▶ *You all feel better – you don't feel resentful and other people don't have to find you've lied to them.*

The myths of being upfront

Why, with the benefits of being honest and direct and the drawbacks of beating around the bush, do we still so often opt for avoidance? There are plenty of myths and beliefs about being upfront. You may feel:

▶ *saying 'No' will upset other people*
▶ *saying 'No' will appear selfish or arrogant*

- ▶ *saying 'No' will inconvenience other people*
- ▶ *saying 'No' will alienate other people.*

Saying 'No' will upset other people. On the contrary, people are more likely to respect and listen to you if you are forthright. What might be upset is their plans which could suffer a setback as they have to do something themselves they had hoped you might do for them. But that's their problem, not yours. They are responsible for their stuff and you are responsible for yours. They shouldn't be trying to make you responsible for theirs and you certainly shouldn't let them get away with it.

Saying 'No' will appear selfish or arrogant. You could more correctly argue it might be seen as selfish and arrogant for someone else to assume you'll jump when they demand it. If you have other plans or simply don't want to do what has been asked, you have every right to say so.

Saying 'No' will inconvenience other people. So it may. But you have to balance up your inconvenience with theirs. Since it was they who decided to involve you without getting your consent, it is actually they who are inconveniencing themselves, not you.

Saying 'No' will alienate other people. If someone demands you do what they require without thinking of your well-being or choice in the matter, and they then become upset at the situation, you may have to ask yourself: should you be putting yourself out for someone who cares so little for you? You don't have to be friends with everyone. Being alienated from someone demanding and destructive may not be such a bad thing, after all.

Insight

To be in a fit state to look after and care for other people we also have to look after and care for ourselves. If we don't, it's a bit like having an empty cup of coffee – when people come asking for a sip, there's nothing left for them. We need to fill our cup of coffee by caring for ourselves so that when those we love do come asking for help, we have enough in our cup to be able to give them some.

Essential points to consider

1 Making excuses only postpones the issue. Other people will still feel free to make the same requests of you in the future.
2 Saying no is neither rude nor unfair.
3 Always being a 'Yes' person does not make you happy and popular. You can become frustrated and resentful and may lose your self-respect and respect from those around you.
4 Strategies such as pre-empting, being honest and direct, or giving a simple 'No' without the need of an explanation can help you make your point.
5 If someone cannot accept a reasonable 'No' from you, do they really have your interests at heart and are they really a friend?

13 tips for saying no

▶ Recognize you have the same rights as everyone else.
▶ Take your time.
▶ Watch your stance.
▶ Watch your body language.
▶ Watch what you say.
▶ Watch your feelings.
▶ Resist the hook.
▶ Put up with the guilt.
▶ Consider the outcome.
▶ Start small.
▶ Recognize it takes time.
▶ Sometimes, say yes.
▶ Don't make it personal.

Recognize you have the same rights as everyone else. Your time, your choices, your wishes and your well-being is every bit as important as theirs. They may feel their wish for you to do what they want is paramount. It isn't. You matter too.

Take your time. If the other person or persons try to hurry you into a decision, take your time. If you know someone is going to ask or expect you to do something you don't want to do, spend some time before seeing them thinking it over. What might they ask? What would you like to do, what would you not want to do? Concentrate on a positive outcome for you both – and remember that giving in may not be as positive for them as they may think. Be clear about what you want to say or achieve by the conversation or encounter. If you don't feel ready, politely but firmly suggest it be undertaken at a later time or date. Say 'If you want the answer now, it's no. If you are prepared to wait while I consider it, it's maybe.'

Watch your stance. If they're sitting, sit down with them. If they're standing, stand up too. If it's a child, or someone in a wheelchair, crouch down. Make eye contact and make sure the person is connecting to you and the conversation by saying their name and if appropriate, touching a hand, arm or leg.

Watch your body language. You don't want to be defensive, nor do you want to be saying you'll do as they ask with the way you appear. Crossing arms, hunching over, turning away all say you're defensive. Smiling while trying to refuse a request gives the answer yes, whatever your words are saying. Turning towards the other person, with your hands in your lap or your arms by side in a relaxed position say you're listening. 'Mirroring' – having the same stance in reverse of the person you're talking – can send the message that you're on the same wavelength. Crowding someone by coming into their personal space is aggressive; standing your ground and allowing someone their space is assertive.

Watch what you say. You don't need to explain yourself. Giving elaborate excuses for why you are not going to do something undercuts your refusal. It tells the other person you think you owe them something. That gives them the opening they need – all they need to do is overcome your excuses by finding another time or place or favour and you'll then say yes.

Watch your feelings and how they are being revealed when you do talk with someone asking you to do something you don't want to do. Clenched fists? Gritted teeth? Are you hunching over, crossing arms, turning away – all signs that you feel vulnerable? If you can see them so can the other person. Take a deep breath and relax, or politely but firmly say you'll stop now and resume at another time.

Resist the hook. People who know you also know how to hook you in by playing on your sense of responsibility or guilt. Every time you say yes when you should have said no, their behaviour is reinforced – that is, they know it works and will do it again. Saying no now sets the scene for being able to say no afterwards. Say yes now and you'll keep on saying it.

Put up with the guilt. When you begin to say no you'll probably feel guilty: you should have said yes, what will they think of you, it won't take a moment... Grit your teeth and accept it. It's only the weight of all those years of being made to feel you should put yourself out speaking. In time, you'll realize you don't have to feel that way at all, and you won't.

Consider the outcome. What could they do if you did say no? And if you were away or ill and couldn't do what is being asked of you, what would they do? What is the worst thing that might happen if you say 'no'? How likely is that to happen?

Start small and gain experience. Say no to something small and unimportant, just to be able to know the sky doesn't fall when you do. Remind yourself of that when you need to say no to something big.

Recognize it takes time. It took years to make you someone who always said yes. It may take months to become someone who can say no when it's appropriate. Celebrate your triumphs, understand your small setbacks and continue the process. It's hard work but it will be worthwhile.

Sometimes, say yes. Once you say no to the things that aren't your responsibility or you can't take on or simply choose not to do, you will learn how to discriminate. Then, you can say yes to things you have the time and inclination to take on or simply choose to do. Once you can say no and are known for it, your yes will be valued all that more. Saying yes all the time doesn't make you valued or liked, it makes you a doormat. Choosing when you will or won't makes you worthwhile.

Don't make it personal. By your words, manner and behaviour make it clear that this isn't about them, it's about you. You aren't saying no because you don't love them, don't like them, don't want to be with them or help them. You're saying no because it doesn't suit you, you don't choose to do it… and that's that.

10 THINGS TO REMEMBER

1   Saying 'Yes' all the time probably means you are taking on too many of other people's responsibilities as well as your own.

2   Being assertive means refusing when necessary but leaving everyone feeling OK about it. This takes time, skill and practice.

3   Avoiding difficulties by using excuses when it should have been a clear 'No' from you doesn't tackle the real problem – it only postpones or prolongs it.

4   It's a myth that when women say 'No' it actually means 'Yes'.

5   Just because you're a parent, you don't always have to put your needs second to those of your family.

6   We all have obligations and responsibilities but these should be mutual or negotiable. You have every right to say 'No' if this delicate balance is not being observed honestly.

7   Just because someone asks you for something doesn't give them priority or privilege. It just means they stepped forward first. You can, just as easily, step back.

8   You will respect and like yourself more if you assert yourself. Being a perpetual 'doormat' will only lead you to frustration and resentment.

9   Be firmly aware that you have the same rights as everyone else – not more, but by no means less.

10 If you are still having doubts about making the necessary effort to assert yourself, ask yourself this question: 'If I never say no to anyone, what's my "Yes" worth?'

QUIZ

1 *Your mum rings for the tenth time that day and asks you to call round on your way home. You have a commitment. Do you say:*
   a No.
   b Sorry Mum, not tonight.
   c Oh, I'd love to but I'm going out at 7 and I'm really going to be in a rush because I've extra work to finish here before I can leave...

2 *You had a meal at your best friend's last weekend and a phone call comes, with a very heavy hint that this weekend it's your turn. Do you say:*
   a No.
   b Can't do it this weekend. Get your diary – let's fix another time.
   c Oh no – that would be great but my other half has just phoned to say we're off to the in-laws tonight for the whole weekend and I'd cancel that like a shot but you know what they're like...

3 *It's Friday, 4.30 and the boss walks in with a two-hour job that he says has to be done tonight, and you've got tickets to an event you've been looking forward to all week. Do you say:*
   a No.
   b It would have been helpful to have had this an hour ago. I'll do an hour and come in early on Monday to finish it.
   c Oh no! Oh dear. Well, I suppose...Can't someone else do it? I've just had a call from home and I have to get back – the baby has come down with a tummy bug and we'll have to get the doctor out and you know how frightened small children can get...

4 *You spot your team leader bearing down on you with a
   determined look on their face, and your schedule is already
   full. Do you say:*
   a *No.*
   b *Before you go any further, you need to know I'm really
      busy and I can't take any extra work on at the moment.*
   c *Don't! I know what you're going to say – I can tell by the
      look on your face! I'm up to my eyes! I can't do another
      thing! Let me show you what I've got to do over the next
      few days…*

5 *Your kids ask you to take them to the shopping centre on
   Saturday. You know you're going to feel awful if you say no, but
   you also know you don't have the time this week. Do you say:*
   a *No.*
   b *Not this week. Let's make a date for next week when
      I have the time.*
   c *Oh god! I don't have the time. No really, I don't – you
      know what I've got on this week and I've got to do all
      those things before Monday and ….*

How did you do?

Mostly As? You're being more aggressive than assertive. It's all
very well being firm and standing your ground and not having to
give excuses. But a few more words make you sound less abrupt
and hostile. Go back and consider your communication skills,
to present a warmer yet still confident front.

Mostly Bs? You've got the knack of being firm and yet welcoming
to the people with whom you interact. They know where they
stand with you and yet don't feel brushed aside or bullied. Read on
to learn even more strategies.

Mostly Cs? You're having some difficulties putting your skills
into practice and still fall back into giving excuses when you don't
need to. You may need to reread and revise to take on board the
suggestions on confidence building and communication skills.

10

....

Getting caught

In this chapter you will learn:
- *hooks – what they are and how they work*
- *about giving away power*
- *whose problem is this, really?*
- *taking back control.*

Knowing that you have the right to say no, and even how to do it, is one thing. Committing yourself to actually doing it is another. And much of the time, what holds you back is a hook. Hooks are those beliefs, habits or pressures that tell you it's up to you to fix whatever problem is presented. Your mum wants someone to talk to? That's you. Your friend needs a baby-sitter? That's you. Your boss needs somebody to do extra work to finish their project? That's you.

_____

Knowing whose responsibility it is

Knowing whose responsibility it is to fix the problem or find a solution is important because it stops you getting caught and trapped in other people's needs and expectations. You need to recognize when those around you are using guilt, myths, manipulation, argument, martyrdom and a host of other 'string-pulls' to get you to do what they want, rather than what you want. They may be doing it deliberately, or they may be using all or some of these without realizing it and without malice.

Whatever, it's worthwhile knowing how pity, compassion, duty or embarrassment lead us to think and say 'I had to do it for her', 'I couldn't get here in time because I couldn't leave', or 'They'd have been upset if I'd said no.'

Case study

Paul and Hayley came to me with, among other issues, disagreements about how much her mother interfered with their marriage. He felt they couldn't settle into a relationship together, and he certainly didn't want to start a family, because of the amount of time she spent with her mother. Since their wedding two years previously, she would call in on her way home from work every day, pop in on Saturday and Sunday lunch was always at her parents' home. More importantly, no decision about their home, their holidays and even the fact they should be having children, was made without her mother having her input. Hayley agreed that her primary home was now with Paul, and that it ought to be the two of them alone who should be making decisions about their life. However, she insisted it was easier said than done. Her mother wouldn't take no for an answer and insisted on her being in as much contact. Hayley felt she could do nothing about it. Significantly, she was persistently late for counselling sessions. A few minutes on the first one, several minutes late most weeks and half an hour late on two occasions. Sometimes they met there, and Paul would always be on time. When they came together, they would be late together and he would be seething. What she was doing here was 'acting out' for me in graphic detail how much this was a problem. It not only interfered with their life, it interfered with their therapy. The last time they were late, I challenged it. Instead of accepting the usual 'Sorry I'm late – couldn't help it, silly me!' I asked her directly, what had made her late? 'Oh, I had to see my mother and she kept me.' Of course, I said. It's really hard when someone locks the door behind you. 'What? Oh no, the door wasn't locked' So, she took your car keys so you couldn't leave? 'No, of course not!' Then, she shackled you to the radiator? Or maybe she threatened to become violent if you left? By now Hayley didn't know whether to laugh or get angry with me. 'No, of course she didn't!' So tell me Hayley, in exactly what way did your mother keep you? You're an adult and you're coming to see a counsellor because of anxieties about your marriage. How – and perhaps as much to the point, why – did your mother stop you leaving? After a lot of discussion Hayley realized that her mum couldn't 'keep her' or 'stop her'. Only Hayley could do that. She was giving her mother the power, handing over control for her own life and choices and for her own self-image. Hayley's mother felt very threatened by the counselling – it was already giving Hayley the idea that perhaps her relationship with her husband should be more central in her life than the relationship with her mother. So of course she wanted Hayley to be late for sessions. But it was up to Hayley to say 'Nice to see you Mum, I'm leaving now' and mean it. Once she realized only she herself had the power to stop herself, or choose to leave, she used it.

Recognizing a hook

Hayley and Paul's story illustrates several important points about being hooked:

▶ *How they do it.*
▶ *How you do it.*
▶ *Why.*

How they do it. In some situations, people may force you to do something you don't want to do with expressed threats. You may genuinely fear they will do harm to you, themselves or other people unless you comply with their demands. But more often, the threat or complaint is implied. If it's a friend or relative, the message may be if you don't do as I say: I'll ... be ill ('Oh, my heart, my heart!'); be disappointed in you; be hurt by you; shout at you; make life unpleasant for you. Guilt and manipulation may be used to make you feel responsible for their well-being, their comfort, their happiness. And clearly, they can only be well, comfortable and happy if you do exactly as they say or expect. A few words or a whole array of non-verbal cues remind you of things said in the past – that you failed them before and surely you can't even be thinking of doing it again? If this is a work colleague, the message may be that you'll be letting down the team, failing in your duties or risking your job unless you do whatever is required.

> ## Insight
> You cannot have power taken away from you. You need to give up control over your actions and decisions for other people to 'make you' do what they want. They can't do it alone. They need you to participate.

How you do it. But – and this is the vital aspect of being hooked – they can't do anything to you that you don't allow them to do. If you're locked in, tied up, have your escape route cut off or are otherwise tangibly restrained or compelled, you clearly have no choice. In all other circumstances, you cannot be made to do anything unless you collude with it. That is not to minimize the pressure and the sheer strength of influence these people may have over you. But it is to say since they can't do it on their own, they need your co-operation, and that therefore you have the power and the choice to say 'No'.

Why. People may tell you at the time that they have only your interests at heart. But the reality is that if guilt or manipulation is being used it is their interests to the fore. It may be their need for company, help or just control. Whatever, it's about them, not you. They may actually and truly believe what they are saying. That's not the point. You are the only judge of your own needs and welfare. Of course, we're always grateful and pleased when family, friends or colleagues share concerns and offer suggestions. But it's up to you to take it or leave it. And while we may often want to be generous with time and attention, sometimes we need to think of ourselves and our own needs. After all, that's what the other person is doing, and you have the same rights as them. Not more perhaps but certainly not less.

> ## Insight
> Imagine the problem being put at your feet as a parcel. When someone calls on you, using an appeal to your role as son or

daughter, friend or colleague, what they seem to be saying is 'I can't handle what's in this parcel – I want you to take it from me and deal with it.' When we come running or stay behind when we really want to leave, what we're doing is picking up the parcel – which immediately leaks mess and smell all over our hands – and taking responsibility for it. We're making the parcel our own, and accepting that dealing with it takes precedence over what we want or need to do. Next time, ask yourself this: Whose parcel is it? Is it mine or this other person's? If it's mine of course I have to open and clear it up. But if it's not my parcel, I don't have to do that. I can refuse to accept it, or hand it back, saying 'Here – this is yours, not mine. Bye!'

The power of the past

A key to the fact that you're being hooked in by guilt and manipulation is that you're not really dealing – or not only dealing – with the here and the now. When someone either deliberately or accidentally hooks you, there are good reasons. You're actually dealing with another time, another circumstance, another place and sometimes another person than the one in front of you at the moment. Sometimes hooks can be that the person openly appeals to another time and place: 'We've always had Sunday lunch as a family!' or 'You used to drop in to see me on your way home when you lived round the corner – why stop just because you're three bus stops away?' Sometimes it's simply that you can remember the angry parent telling you off when you were a child, and you don't want to risk hearing that again. And often, when work colleagues or some people you meet pull rank on you, you feel like a child with an angry parent or angry teacher again, and slip into behaving accordingly.

When you feel compelled to do something that either you don't want to do or on reflection is going to cause problems in your life – conflict with a partner, diverting your attention away from your own close family, making extra and unjustified labour for you at work – ask yourself the following:

- ▶ *How do I feel?*
- ▶ *When did I feel like this before?*
- ▶ *How old am I?*
- ▶ *Where am I?*
- ▶ *Who am I speaking to?*

How do I feel? Do you feel powerless and out of control? Angry, rejected, scared, upset, panicky? Close your eyes and put your finger on exactly the emotion, or emotions, that affect you at this moment. You may at first have difficulty identifying it, or them, because they may seem contradictory or out of proportion. Why on earth, you may tell yourself, would I feel on the edge of panic because a friend wants me to baby-sit and I have other things I need to do? If you sift through your emotions honestly, you may allow yourself to recognize it really is anxiety, and this is pushing you to say yes when you really want to say no.

When did I feel like this before? Once you know what you're feeling, you can usually cast your mind back to when you've felt like that before. Being told 'Bad child! What a disappointment you are!' by a parent, grandparent or teacher? Having a partner turn away from you because you didn't do as they wanted, and they made you feel terrible and to blame for that? When you locate how you've felt before you can often see that what you're feeling now has as much, if not more, to do with that echo. Your earlier feelings are being repeated and multiplying how you might properly and appropriately react to what is going on now.

How old am I? The emotions that drive you to accept being manipulated are powerful. It is often feelings we had as children that have that particular ability to flood you, making thinking clearly difficult. An interesting and useful strategy is to ask yourself how old your inner self is when you feel this way. Ask, and an age is likely to pop into your head. Once you know how old you feel you also can realize how much that can contribute to your difficulties. As a grown adult maybe you should be able to resist the manipulation you are experiencing. But how can an eight-year-old do so? That's the age at which you are functioning.

Where am I? As well as being taken to an emotional state, a time and an age, your unconscious mind may also be taking you back to a place. Being carpeted by the boss may summon up irresistible but barely realized memories of being sent to the head when you were at school. All that helpless embarrassment you suffered then may still be tying your tongue and clouding your mind.

Who am I speaking to? When you find yourself feeling you 'have to' do certain things or 'can't leave', 'can't say no', whose voice do you hear telling you this is so? Is it a relative, a teacher, someone else? Is it the person you're with but from a different time or someone else entirely?

The answers to these five questions can give you some insight into exactly why you might find it so hard to shake off the influence of those around you. They have hooks to pull and buttons to press, and sometimes they know exactly what they are doing. But the important thing to note is this. While you are in ignorance of what is going on, it's easy for them to pressure you, and hard for you to fight back. Once you realize exactly what is happening and why – what you feel, what it reminds you of – it becomes much harder for them to have quite that authority over you, and far easier for you to stand firm.

Insight

Once you can understand a hook you can recognize you're in the here and now, not in the past. When you can deal with what is happening at the time and resist any extra emotional influence, you may find it far easier to respond with your own needs and interests at heart. You are responsible for your stuff – they, not you, are responsible for theirs.

1   'Hooks' –beliefs, habits or pressures – pull you
    into feeling that it's up to you to fix other people's
    problems.
2   Ask yourself 'Whose problem is it really?' If it's not
    yours, hand it back saying 'Here – it's yours not mine.'
3   Putting your finger on what you feel and what it
    reminds you of can help you resist a hook.

Countering hooks

When you feel a situation is getting out of your control and
you're being asked or expected to do too much or things that you
don't want to do, take a deep breath and sit down. Ask yourself
those five questions and listen to the answers. Simply recognizing
the hooks helps. But one by one you can work through them,
countering each one. You can tell yourself:

▶ *My emotion may be anger/panic/anxiety but that may not be
   a feeling of the moment. That puts me in control.*
▶ *I might have felt anger/panic/anxiety then. I don't have to, now.
   That puts me in control.*
▶ *I might be remembering being eight. I'm an adult now and
   I don't have to feel helpless. That puts me in control.*
▶ *I might be taken back in my memories to somewhere else but
   I'm here, now. That puts me in control.*
▶ *I'm not the same person as I was then and the person I'm
   speaking to is not the same as in my memory. That puts me
   in control.*

What Hayley recognized was that she had a clear choice – to be her mother's daughter or her husband's partner. Her mother couldn't really 'make her' stay or 'keep her' from leaving. Her mother had no power to 'force her' to go round every day. Her mother could ask, demand, make a fuss. But it was Hayley who did the going and the staying. It was not only a choice she had to make, it was a choice she was already acting on. By being 'helpless' she was choosing to ally with her mother. Which was fine, if that was what she wanted to do. It wasn't. We went through the five questions, identified exactly what was going on. Having discussed the situation, she practised counters to each one. Hayley loved her mother, and told her so. She also told her from then on she would be phoning more often than calling in, that Saturday was a family day for her and Paul, and Sunday lunch was no longer a 'given' – sometimes her parents would be invited to her house, sometimes she and Paul would accept an invitation to go to theirs but it would no longer be every week. By claiming her ability to make such decisions over issues to do with her mother, Hayley also found herself far more confident at work, and her and Paul's relationship improved.

CASE STUDY

Insight

It's very easy to get into the mindset that tells you that you don't have choices. You're so busy that all you can manage are the things that have to be done; you're so under pressure from other people that you simply must do as they ask. You may be busy, you may be under pressure but the simple truth is that you can make the choice to say no, to do what you want rather than what you 'have' to do. You're making a choice now – to react to outside demands. Make another choice – to act on your own preferences.

10 THINGS TO REMEMBER

1 *Learn to recognize the 'hooks' – the beliefs, habits and pressures that can keep you saying 'Yes' to everything.*

2 *'Whose parcel is it?' can help you recognize whose problem this really is. If it's not yours, it's not your responsibility to fix it.*

3 *You may choose to help someone solve their problem. That still doesn't make it yours.*

4 *'I only have your interests at heart' may be true on occasions. But if guilt or manipulation is being used on you, it is always the other person's interests that are to the fore.*

5 *Hooks work by bringing feelings from the past into the here and now.*

6 *If your reaction seems out of proportion, ask yourself exactly what you feel at that moment, and use the strategies we've discussed to explain why.*

7 *Once you can put your finger on exactly the emotions you are feeling, you will be better equipped to interpret and deal with the situation you find yourself in.*

8 *When reacting to pressure, ask yourself how old you actually feel inside. Is it childhood memories that are influencing you?*

9 *Once you are able to understand what is happening to you and why, it will become far easier for you to resist or counter a hook.*

10 *Consider the situations in which you feel 'I have to' and see how many you would like to move into the 'I choose to' category, or say 'No' to.*

In what situations do you find yourself saying 'I can't...', 'I have to...', 'I must...'? When can you look after yourself, and do things you choose to do? Write down as many as you can think of:

I have to:	I choose to:

Consider all the items you've put in 'I have to…'. Which ones would you like to move from the left hand to the right hand column?

About each one ask yourself the five questions:

1 *How do I feel?*
2 *When did I feel like this before?*
3 *How old am I?*
4 *Where am I?*
5 *Who am I speaking to?*

Run through all the assertive techniques we have rehearsed. Which ones can you now move from the left hand to the right hand column?

11

Anger and other feelings

In this chapter you will learn:
- *about recognizing and naming emotions and feelings*
- *understanding and controlling your emotions and feelings*
- *how feelings, behaviour and needs are linked.*

As we saw in Chapter 6, becoming assertive requires thought. While there may be many things we do in life that we do instinctively and automatically, such as breathing, assertiveness has to be learnt and practised. You start out as a total beginner and learner and end up proficient, passing through the four stages of competence:

▶ *Unconscious Incompetence. You can't do it and don't know that you can't do it.*
▶ *Conscious Incompetence. You can't do it and you do know you can't do it.*
▶ *Conscious Competence. You can do it, and know so, but have to concentrate on what you are doing.*
▶ *Unconscious Competence. You don't know you know it – it's now second nature.*

Up until the last stage, when it has become something you do effortlessly, becoming assertive is likely to be something we need to consider and focus on. It becomes easier as we make the techniques and strategies our own and as they begin to pay off. Nothing makes learning and practising easier than seeing how it works and benefits us, and those around us. Forgetting to think and focus can hold us back. So too can emotions.

Naming emotions

We all have emotions. Some are pleasant and thus felt to be positive: joy, love, pride. Some are less so: embarrassment, disappointment, anxiety. Some are really disagreeable and so felt to be negative: anger, jealousy, despair. We often struggle with naming our emotions – we can confuse fear with anger, lust with love. Most important of all, we frequently try to push away emotions we'd rather not have, or think are contradictory or 'wrong' for the time and place.

> **Insight**
>
> Anger and jealousy are often felt to be emotions we shouldn't have. Such negative, hostile feelings are seen as not only unpleasant but unnatural. There is a myth that somehow we should rise above them and should curb or deny them. This often starts in childhood. 'You shouldn't feel jealous of your little sister!'; 'What an angry face – what a bad child!'

The myths about feelings

Consider the times you have tried to be calm, logical and practise your assertiveness skills, only to be thrown into disarray. You try to serenely go through the 'When... I feel... Because... What I would like...' sequence. Instead you find yourself screaming 'Clean up your bloody mess! I'm not your servant!' Again. As usual. Why? Because a powerful emotion got between you and your thinking processes. And it's probably there because you haven't been able to face up to it, because the myths about feelings make it hard to pin them down and deal with them.

Case study

Shelly got in touch because she and her fiancé Adam were 'going through a rough patch'. He expressed enormous anger and frustration at the fact that Shelly would never argue. He'd bring up something he felt they needed to discuss, and she would close down and avoid the issue to the extent of staying late at work rather than coming home and talking to him. She would also stay up late watching television until he'd gone to bed, and fallen asleep. Shelly said she just didn't like arguing – her parents never argued and she found it distasteful. When we explored what she actually felt, it emerged that Shelly was actually a very angry person. But the message she'd got from her parents was that anger was wrong; it was dirty and unseemly and anyone feeling it was bad. She was terrified of her anger – she thought if she finally expressed it, the sky would fall. Young children feel their anger is scarily powerful and are often terrified that expressing anger would hurt them and their parents. Indeed, Shelly was sure if she did show anger, Adam would leave her. The result of her burying her anger, however, wasn't that it went away. Her anger came out in punishing silences – and painful headaches. It took some time for her to be able to access and express her feelings but when she did, she found she felt better, Adam wasn't shocked and their relationship improved.

What are the myths about feelings?

- ▶ *It's bad to have bad feelings.*
- ▶ *Having bad feelings makes you a bad person.*
- ▶ *You should be able to control your feelings.*

It's bad to have bad feelings. We tend to believe that destructive emotions are dangerous and that we really shouldn't have them. They harm us, they harm those around us and so the desirable situation is to banish them. Indeed, we sometimes extend this to cover even powerful 'good' emotions such as love. At the wrong time, for the wrong person, you really shouldn't be feeling like that!

Having bad feelings makes you a bad person. This follows on from the first belief – if it's bad to feel that way, feeling that way makes you a bad person. And that, of course, is why we tend to hide from, deny and avoid naming or understanding the emotions we have. We fear that if we admit to ourselves we are experiencing jealousy or anger, it means we are horrible people.

You should be able to control your feelings. If it's bad to feel and feeling makes you bad, inevitably we assume we should be able to turn off emotions like a tap. You don't want to be a bad person; you don't want to think of yourself as bad. So, you assume you can avoid being so and doing so by controlling or denying what you feel.

Insight

Feelings are feelings. In themselves they are neither good nor bad – they are just feelings. We all have them, and for a reason.

Needs, feelings and behaviour

Feelings are a vital component in the needs/feelings/behaviour cycle. Needs lead to feelings and feelings lead to behaviour.

We all have needs. Common needs might be for:

▶ *attention*
▶ *respect*
▶ *love*
▶ *security*
▶ *safety*
▶ *acceptance*
▶ *independence.*

We have them as babies, as children and as adults. If you can imagine a fountain, needs bubble around under the surface, like water in the bowl.

We want those needs to be fulfilled, and so they give rise to our feelings which act as a signal of what we require, and of whether our needs are being fulfilled or not. We can have feelings such as:

▶ *joy*
▶ *happiness*
▶ *sadness*

- ▶ *moodiness*
- ▶ *anger*
- ▶ *hurt*
- ▶ *fear*
- ▶ *jealousy*
- ▶ *confidence*
- ▶ *self-esteem*
- ▶ *pride*.

Think of that fountain. With our needs under the surface, the feelings spurt, gush and trickle out, like jets of water from the bowl. Those feelings are the result of our needs and the visible sign of them. The problem is that we don't always link the need under the surface to the emotion we experience. When we don't understand what we need, we can't explain to others. And when our needs are unfulfilled, feelings of anger and frustration can grow.

Imagine the situation of a teenager who wants to go to a concert with friends. You have said no and your teenager screams 'I hate you! All my friends are going! You're ruining my life!'

What a loss of fuss, you think. How rude and undisciplined!

Think of that fountain. What might be in the bowl? Needs: for respect, acceptance, attention from friends? For love, security, safety from you?

So what might the teenager be thinking? Not 'I hate you' but 'I'll be left out – all my friends will think I'm a loser!' The fountain of feelings spurting out may then be jealousy, anger, fear.

And what is the behaviour? Read on…

....

Insight

You don't get rid of powerful emotions by repressing them. What actually happens is that they simmer under the surface and eventually burst out, often in surprising and confusing ways.

(Contd)

Anger may come out as self-loathing or despair. Shyness or the need for acceptance may come out as jealousy. By pushing them under, these feelings often multiply, emerging far more powerfully or violently than if acknowledged and voiced earlier on. It's similar to what happens when a child falls and suffers a dirty graze. If you cleaned it at once it might hurt but it would heal. Hide it and cover it up and it will fester. It may be out of sight but the result is far more destructive.

Which is where behaviour comes in. Behaviour is what adults and children do as a result of those feelings, to try to meet their needs. Often we're not aware of what we need and what we do or say may not be a very successful way of getting our need met at all. It may end up upsetting other people as well.

In this situation, for instance, the behaviour is slammed doors, shouting, fighting and even truanting. Because what are the child's feelings? They're probably anger and resentment and maybe even fear. And what's the need? It's likely to be for attention or for acceptance and the respect of the peer group. Underneath the behaviour are feelings – under the feelings are needs.

Understanding feelings and needs

Sometimes it's hard to recognize what we do need in a particular situation – it may be attention, it may be respect, it may be unconditional love. Our feelings can help us work this out. Having your needs met brings happiness, joy, satisfaction. When we don't get what we need we may feel sad, angry or upset.

Feelings aren't right or wrong – they just are. But the way people react to their feelings can be confusing or upsetting. It helps if you can:

▶ *see feelings as a warning sign of needs*
▶ *recognize everyone's feelings and needs are important, even if they can't expect to have them satisfied all the time*

- *share feelings rather than bury them until they burst out*
- *learn to put names to your own and your family's feelings and needs*

Being aware of the link between feelings, needs and behaviour can help us. We can 'dive under' what we find ourselves saying or doing to try to get a sense of the feelings and needs underneath in order to understand ourselves and let other people know clearly how we feel and what we need. That way, when you find yourself about to lose track of the calm, assertive manner you were about to bring to bear on the situation and instead let rip, you can pull back. You can ask yourself:

- *What's my need?*
- *What's my feeling?*
- *What's my behaviour?*

When you're dealing with someone else who is being difficult, you can ask yourself:

- *What might be their need?*
- *What might be their feeling?*
- *What's their behaviour?*

Your answers can help you address the situation with more control.

10 THINGS TO REMEMBER

1   *Assertiveness has to be learnt and practised – it is not instinctive or automatic.*

2   *Nothing makes learning and practising easier than seeing how things work and how they can benefit you.*

3   *Understanding the four stages of competence and their effects can start you on your journey to assertiveness.*

4   *We often struggle with recognizing, or naming correctly, our emotions and feelings.*

5   *Don't automatically push away feelings you feel are 'bad' or that you would rather not have.*

6   *Try to bury or deny 'bad' feelings or emotions and they will still emerge.*

7   *Needs lead to feelings and feelings lead to behaviour.*

8   *Behaviour is what we do to meet our needs. We don't behave badly – we behave in ways that indicate our needs.*

9   *Recognizing underlying needs can help you modify or challenge behaviour.*

10 *Ask yourself 'What's the need, the feeling, the behaviour?' when you are faced with difficult or challenging situations.*

QUIZ

1 *I feel angry:*
   a *Often but I bottle it up.*
   b *Rarely but when I do I try to work out why and deal with it.*
   c *Sometimes and it's when people annoy me.*

2 *If I lose my temper with someone:*
   a *I feel guilty.*
   b *I apologize and move on.*
   c *I know it must have been about something they did.*

3 *When children behave badly:*
   a *I try to see what I must have done to set them off.*
   b *I try to understand the feeling under the behaviour and the need under the feeling.*
   c *I know it's because they're naughty.*

4 *When other people are upset:*
   a *I try to fix it.*
   b *I'll help if I can but their feelings are their responsibility.*
   c *I leave them to it – it's their business.*

How did you do?

Mostly As? You're still taking responsibility for other people's feelings. You might like to read the previous chapter again.

Mostly Bs? You're coming along on the journey, recognizing that emotions are natural and normal and a guide to whether our needs are being met. Read on for more support in your quest for assertiveness.

Mostly Cs? You see emotions as dangerous, and other people as the cause of any difficulties between you. You need to balance an assertive recognition of responsibility with a tendency to blame others. You need to look again at what we've discussed on communication skills and emotions.

12

Changing others by changing yourself

In this chapter you will learn:
- *how others may react to your new assertiveness*
- *about changing other people by changing yourself*
- *about negotiating and making contracts.*

Because of the way we have evolved, we incline towards fight or flight. Both have survival implications in a more primitive time. But in a world where we increasingly find the best survival tactic is co-operation, where we protect our own and other people's interests together instead of seeking to dominate and overcome, assertive behaviour is important.

Insight
Whatever may seem to happen, the truth is that neither the meek nor the bullies inherit the world: those who value teamwork do.

Your assertiveness impacts on those around you

Becoming more assertive means inevitably that you impact on those around you. The people whose behaviour led to your wanting to learn how to assert yourself in the first place – family or friends, work colleagues or people you encounter in public – will react to the new you. Their response may be welcoming and positive. With your new found self-esteem and confidence, recognizing how much this benefits you, you may want to spread the advantages around to those you know. Or, of course, they may react with surprise or even hostility.

Passing on what you have learnt has two returns. One is that it helps those around you to deal with your assertiveness, and makes life a lot easier for you. The second is that it helps them become more assertive themselves.

There is, however, a catch. The reality is that you cannot change other people. You may want to do so, and hope that by demanding it or wishing it, they will see the sense of what you are asking and do as you ask. It doesn't happen that way. You can't force behaviour change on other people. Their behaviour and their beliefs are their responsibility, not yours. But by being assertive yourself you can show them how assertive behaviour is a helpful model to follow.

Case study

Janice came to me with a shopping list of changes she wanted. She wanted her husband to stop being so bossy with her. 'For instance, he won't let me drive when we go out together even though he's the one always having prangs – my licence is clean.' She wanted her sons to do as they were told – clean their rooms, stop fighting and do homework when asked. She wanted her mother to stop calling her 20 times a day. She wanted her best friend to stop dumping her problems on her and always asking for help but never offering it. I said I'd love to wave a magic wand and do that all for her, but I couldn't. And neither could she. None of us can change other people. The only person who can do that is them. What we can do, however, is change ourselves. 'But I don't need to change! They're the ones making life difficult for me!' said Janice. Let's see, I said.

Changing others by changing yourself

We often wish we could change the people with whom we have conflict or who intimidate us. If only they would change, we think, we'd be all right. We wouldn't have to work at being assertive and our troubles would be over. It's other people who seem to be the problem – why can't they be different?

There are several problems with this approach. One is that by seeking to change other people, we make them accountable, and thus in control, for how we feel and how we act. That may not be the real issue. It may be our approach that needs to alter. And whether it is us or them at the root of it, we should always accept that it is we who are responsible for our own feelings and actions. It is the last reason that is the most important. That is, that since we can never bank on someone else changing for our convenience, it's not an effective way of seeking to make things better.

It might feel comfortable and handy to blame someone else for the situation or our emotions. That's a very human way of doing it. But isn't it actually better to take charge? If you accept it might be down to you, you are then in control of turning it all around. Instead of being a victim, you're in control. When it comes down to it, it doesn't really matter whether other people or you are to blame, what matters is that it improves. And since you can get on with streamlining and improving on your own, without having to persuade or wait for others to be ready, taking responsibility for yourself and your changes is simply so effective.

There is yet one more advantage to taking on the work of being different yourself rather than insisting other people should do it. That is what I call the see-saw principle.

The see-saw principle

Imagine you are on a see-saw or teeter-totter. You stand at one end and someone else stands at the other and since you're both the same weight the see-saw is hovering, level and parallel to the ground. Now imagine you would like to move further in towards the centre. So you shout at the other person to move too. They ignore you. So what do you do? Go on shouting? Blame them?

Get angry? This is what we do when we insist that other people have to be different for everything to be better.

What you can do is start moving yourself, to make a small, careful changes for yourself. As you inch forwards, the see-saw starts to unbalance and you might both fall off. But what is likely to happen is that the other person will start shifting forwards too, to balance your move and keep on the level. That is what being assertive can do for you, your friends, family, work colleagues and acquaintances: you move and they move whether they realize it or intend to or not.

Insight

By using the tools of assertiveness, you can get a sense of being in charge of situations, rather than being a victim of what other people want. You can also change the way they behave and feel. Your actions rub off on and affect them, too. You begin the change, but the other person will almost certainly follow your lead.

How does your behaviour affect others?

▶ *You make yourself less of a target.*
▶ *You make yourself a model.*

You make yourself less of a target

People who try to dominate or manipulate you tend to be people with issues themselves. Harmful behaviour patterns such as these come from lack of self-esteem and self-confidence. Which means to make themselves feel better they usually go for the easy target – the person who will back down and follow their lead, to make them feel in charge. To make themselves feel tall, they cut you down to size. It doesn't actually take much to tip the balance into making it clear they'd be better off going elsewhere. And, by your attitude and behaviour you also pass on the message that being self-confident and assertive is an improved and improving way of acting so why not try it?

Imagine yourself as a mugger. You're out on the streets looking for someone to rob.

- *The first person comes along, shuffling with head down and arms crossed, bag hanging off their shoulder.*
- *The second person comes along, walking head down but bag across their body.*
- *The third person comes along, walking head up, arms swinging with bag across their body.*
- *The fourth person comes along, head up and striding along, carrying a stick.*
- *The fifth person comes along, head up and striding along, carrying a stick with a Rottweiler trotting besides them.*

Now – which one are you going to attack?

The easier you make it for other people to attack you, the more they come back to do so. The harder you make it, the more they not only leave you alone but learn something too.

Case study

Dave says 'I had this guy at work and he was always having a go at me. It did feel like very hard work at first. I just plugged away at doing broken record and "I" messages and just getting back the usual stuff – jokes and hassle. It just felt so stupid to be dutifully saying "When... I feel... because... what I would like". Then one day, he just said "Oh. All right." It felt like the sun had come out! I thanked him, he thanked me, and to be honest it's been plain sailing ever since.'

Helping other people become assertive too

For you to really get the best out of an encounter, you and the other person both should be acting assertively. If the other person is:

- ▶ *being aggressive, they won't be listening to your views or needs*
- ▶ *being submissive, they won't be expressing their views*
- ▶ *being passive-aggressive, they may be avoiding any real dialogue.*

By encouraging them to listen, to express their views or by engaging them in the discussion, you not only continue to be assertive yourself, you help them to move out of their dysfunctional behaviour and join you in being effective and co-operative.

Insight

Being assertive is like offering a deal at a car boot sale. You may think the other person has no intention of adjusting their price – and so might they! But you come forwards and negotiate and it actually makes it hard for them not to fall in line with you. When you act assertively rather than fight or flee, the chances are that the other person will follow your pattern.

What you can do is:

- ▶ *explain what you want and invite them to do the same*
- ▶ *put forward potential solutions or ideas and invite them to do the same*
- ▶ *you may need also to point out the consequence of each set of actions, which of course includes the choice of doing none of the actions discussed*
- ▶ *you both assess the idea to see if it meets both your needs. If not, brainstorm other ideas*
- ▶ *if you exhaust all ideas, agree how you will both compromise to find a solution that partly satisfies both of you*
- ▶ *choose a solution that meets both sets of needs.*

It is your responsibility to:

- ▶ *resist giving in to the other person's needs, which would be being unassertive*

- *take account of the other person's needs, because ignoring them would be being aggressive*
- *refuse to go silent or withdraw, which would be being passive-aggressive.*

It is not your responsibility to:

- *put the other person's needs above yours*
- *take on the job of looking after their needs*
- *feel that if they can't 'get it' it's your fault.*

How would you bring this to bear on a dilemma that you are experiencing involving other people? Try filling in this chart.

It helps to see where you and the other person are coming from – what might be your own and the other person's stance and how that could be affecting the situation. Once you do, you can take the discussion to them and using your toolbox of strategies, talk over your shared dilemma, what solutions there might be and what consequences.

Case study

What Janice discovered was that by making changes in her own beliefs, attitudes and behaviour, those around her also began to act differently. She told her husband since it was foolish to drive after drinking, in future they'd share the driving and which one of them could have a drink. The next time they went out, she simply picked up her car keys and said 'My turn.' Her calm confidence said this was not negotiable, and he didn't argue. She instituted a regular Family Roundtable and Family Rules, with a sharp reduction in family squabbles. She told her mother she loved her but she only had time for one call a day and would screen her calls. And she asked her friend for help, giving her the chance to be a helper rather than a victim. 'I can't believe how much everyone else has improved!' she said. 'But I can see it. It's me who started it, isn't it?'

What is your dilemma?	How are you behaving? (Assertive, unassertive, aggressive, passive-aggressive?)	How are other people behaving? (Assertive, unassertive, aggressive, passive-aggressive?)	What solutions might there be?	What might be the consequences?	What strategies and techniques might you use in discussion? (Broken record, 'I' messages, When...)

Using assertiveness with children

It probably goes without saying that you'll want to use your newly honed assertiveness skills in dealing with any children you have. Family conflict, after all, is often the most keenly felt incentive for seeking such skills. What you may not have immediately recognized is that helping your children be assertive themselves may be one of the best tactics to solve such difficulties.

When you help children be self-confident and assertive and to manage their own problems in dealing with other people as well as with you, you often see a marked reduction in family arguments. Since assertiveness is not about trying to dominate others but to resist those who seek to dominate and manipulate you, teaching it to children does not encourage them be aggressive, loud, or bullying. By giving them the skills to resist, of course, it does mean you will have to keep on your toes; you may not be able to dominate them anymore. You will, however, be able to draw boundaries and insist on necessary rules being kept. But you'll do it by proving a good model and asking them to buy into those rules rather than simply throwing your weight around.

Insight

An American family counsellor, Jane Nelson, had, to me, the most persuasive explanation of why sharing assertiveness works with children. She said 'Where did we ever get the crazy idea that in order to make children do better, first we have to make them feel worse? Think of the last time you felt humiliated or treated unfairly. Did you feel like co-operating or doing better?' Playing fair works as well with children as it can with adults. It takes extra work at first, but it saves time in the long run.

Negotiating

One of the key skills in being assertive is negotiating. When you're being dominant, passive or passive-aggressive, you're either laying down the law, having it laid down for you or taking instruction but complaining and planning how to get round it. All of these can lead to arguments and objections, from both sides. Being assertive means having negotiation as your default mode.

WHY NEGOTIATE?

Taking the time to negotiate:

▶ *takes the win/lose out of the situation – everyone gains*
▶ *increases trust and willingness to co-operate; when people know you'll listen to them, they'll listen to you, and when you do have to say no they'll accept it was for a good reason and that you will agree to something they want another day*
▶ *increases mutual understanding and reduces frustration; taking your time and showing respect lowers the temperature and helps others to ask questions and listen in a calm atmosphere*

► sets up a format for dealing with disagreements and conflict;
    once you have tried it and it has worked, you all know the
    rules for subsequent discussions and agreements.

You may think, particularly in your role as a parent, you shouldn't
be negotiating as it shows weakness and parents should always be
in charge. The reality is that negotiation is always more effective
than one person giving orders, and is the assertive option. Saying
'Because I say so!' may work with small children. As they grow up,
it becomes less effective. So how can you negotiate?

HOW TO NEGOTIATE

The key rules for negotiating are:

► *Talk when everyone is calm.*
► *Gather information.*
► *Listen to the other person's views as well.*
► *Be clear about what is (and is not) negotiable.*
► *Pick your battles.*
► *Make an agreement.*
► *Review agreements regularly.*
► *Say thank you!*

Talk when everyone is calm
Pick a neutral space and a time. If this is a family discussion,
choose a time when everyone is relaxed such as over a family
meal or a cup of coffee. Aim to give each of you time to have
your say and listen to the other side without feeling rushed or
pressured. Deferring the discussion until you're in a neutral spot
also gives you the chance to think it through beforehand. For
example, if your son says 'I'm not doing homework tonight!', or
your mother calls and says 'It's a family Sunday lunch this week!',
or a friend says 'I need you to look after my toddler for me this
afternoon!' you *act*, don't react. Open the door to negotiation by
acknowledging what has been said in a neutral way: 'You don't
want to do homework/You want us to come for Sunday lunch this
weekend/You want me to look after Fred this afternoon. Let's get
a cup of coffee/make supper/give me ten minutes and I'll call you

back, and we'll sit down and discuss it.' Stay non-committal and take the time you need to think about how you feel.

Gather information
Once everyone is sitting down say, 'You don't want to do your homework/You'd like us to come to lunch/You want me to look after your toddler. I'd like to hear more and talk about it.' Ask for more information and listen. Take time to think about how you feel about the situation and what information you need to make your decision. If they are pushing you for an answer, say that you can give them a 'No' quickly, but if they want your agreement to something, you need time to talk it through.

Listen to the other person's views as well
In a discussion, to reach a settlement that everyone is happy with, it's important that both sides feel they have been heard, even if they don't get all that they want. Swap between listening and acknowledging the other person's feelings and needs, and stating your own. When making your feelings known, use 'I' messages to put your point across. Instead of saying 'No!' or 'I hate doing that!' say 'I can see what you're saying/asking but it doesn't suit me at the moment.' Be prepared to hear the other person's feelings and needs underneath their words. It may be 'I'm just not in a fit state after school to do my homework, I need a break!' or 'I'm really missing you and need some company' or 'I'm at the end of my tether!'

Insight
When you're dealing with someone who is upset or angry, make it clear that their feelings and needs are important to you. Be aware that if anyone becomes 'emotionally flooded', that is, so upset they can't think straight or express themselves, you may need to call a 'time out' and come back to the discussion later.

Be clear about what is (and is not) negotiable
You might like to make it clear from the start what issues you can and will budge on – and those that you can't and won't. Dropping other important commitments just because the person demanding your attention feels their needs are more important may not work

for you. Accepting any relaxation on safety or health rules – letting kids go to a party where there may be a genuine risk of violence or being driven by someone who drinks and drives could be something non-negotiable. So too may be avoiding homework simply because they don't feel like doing it, or your helping out because your friend fancies yet another day off to go shopping.

Pick your battles

When you negotiate, focus on the issues that really matter.
If you let go on small things you can stand firm when you need to. Negotiating takes time and can feel messy while you are in the middle of it. You may find yourself thinking 'I can't be bothered with this.' But negotiating is actually quicker than a whole saga of shouting, slamming down phones, sulking, and having feuds. You may be tempted to think 'It was so much simpler when I insisted – or gave in for a quiet life!' It might have been simpler, but it was far less pleasant in the long run as resentment and frustration spoiled the atmosphere.

Make an agreement

Once you've gathered in all the information you need, heard the feelings and opinions of the other person and been satisfied they have heard yours too, come to an agreement. Sometimes a conflict is about needs and beliefs. For example, you and your mother may never agree on the belief that every adult child still has to come to Sunday lunch every week or the world will come to an end, or your teenager and you that homework is a waste of time. What you can do is discuss and agree to differ on your opposing beliefs, then negotiate agreements around behaviour so that important needs of everyone can be met with some compromise. You may agree on 'OK – no homework tonight/until you've had a chance to recharge. But it has to be done so what we've agree is you'll do it later/tomorrow.' Or 'Love you Mum but this weekend is for us as a family. I'll ring you on Monday and we'll fix up coming next weekend. Why don't you call that friend of yours?'

Check out that the agreement meets your and the other person's needs and that the outcome is acceptable to you both. And check out that you both have the same understanding of what has been agreed.

One way of doing this is to have a contract. State clearly – or even write down – exactly what you and the other person have said will be done. Work out a fair exchange and one that you can both agree on. Make a precise record of the decision, including:

▶ *what you've both agreed to do*
▶ *how you agree to do it*
▶ *when you agree to do it by*
▶ *for how long you have agreed to do this.*

Review agreements regularly
Review such arrangements regularly. If the terms of the agreement are not being met, discuss why and whether the contract needs to be redrawn or whether something needs to be adjusted. When you're getting used to being assertive and so are the people around you they might slip back into old habits, or even feel the need to test boundaries from time to time. Be prepared to stand firm unless it's time to review the agreement.

Say thank you!
Everyone co-operates when they feel good about it. The more comfortable you become with being assertive, the more confident and self-assured you are, the better other people will also feel about the relationships they have with you. If you thank them for co-operating, and frequently tell them you appreciate what they are doing, they have every incentive for repeating that behaviour. Whether it is family, friends or work colleagues, if most of your encounters are positive and enabling rather than hostile or conflicted you give them a motivation for wanting to interact in this way with you rather than it being a power struggle. If you share opinions in a positive, caring atmosphere when you do need to resolve an issue, the practice gained in being positive helps you to focus on feelings and needs, and swap between listening and expressing yourself, on the route to a resolution.

Insight
Remember to model the behaviour you want back. Say please and thank you, listen and be sympathetic. When people feel respected and heard, they will usually do as you ask.

Pass on the skills

Teaching and modelling assertiveness skills can make family life so much easier for everyone. When children squabble what often happens is they come to you, to be referee or to manage the negative emotions for them. When you continually act as the mediator, settling the rows, this means they never have to learn how to cope for themselves. It works far better to hand over responsibility to them.

▶ *State the problem – 'I see two children arguing over which programme to watch.'*
▶ *State your expectation – 'I think you can sort this out yourselves in a way that suits you both.'*
▶ *State what will happen – 'I'm going to leave you here and you'll come to me in ten minutes and tell me what you've agreed between you.'*

If they can't agree, send them back again. Point out nobody wins if they can't agree, and that it must be a mutually satisfying arrangement.

You'll be surprised how often kids at loggerheads once expected to negotiate and compromise will do so. It's all in the expectation!

Essential points to consider

1 *Helping children be assertive themselves could be one of the best tactics to helping you be assertive with them.*
2 *Negotiation allows you to change win/lose arguments into win/win solutions where both parties are happy with the result.*
3 *Prioritize. Don't give the same weight and intensity to an argument about what music a teenager plays as you would to whether they can get a lift home from someone who has been drinking.*
4 *Once a mutually acceptable solution has been reached, make an agreement or a contract.*

10 THINGS TO REMEMBER

1 *Neither the weak nor the strong inherit the world – those who negotiate and use teamwork do.*

2 *You cannot change other people.*

3 *Other people can change themselves and often do if you start the process.*

4 *Being assertive means that you become less of a target for the unassertive behaviour of others.*

5 *Listening is all important.*

6 *You are responsible for your own behaviour, feelings and needs.*

7 *You are not responsible for the behaviour, feelings and needs of others.*

8 *Be assertive with children and encourage them to be assertive in return.*

9 *Pick your battles and only focus on the issues that really matter.*

10 *Say 'Thank you' when people do co-operate – it gives them an incentive to do so again.*

KEY QUESTIONS FOR CONSIDERING WAYS TO RESOLVE DIFFICULT DILEMMAS

Here is a checklist you might like to use when getting ready to tackle any dilemma or discussion. You can also use this as a chance to review earlier chapters to give you more confidence in what you are doing.

Are you listening?

▶ *What do you want to say – do you need to sit down and think it over?*
▶ *Are you clear what other people are saying – have you checked this out with each person?*
▶ *What do you feel? Are you clear about your feelings?*
▶ *What is everyone else feeling? Are they clear about your feelings? Have you checked?*

What does everyone need and want?

▶ *Is there a conflict between what different people need and want?*
▶ *Has each person been given opportunities to express their needs and wants?*

Who is responsible?

▶ *Who makes the decision?*
▶ *Who sees it through?*
▶ *Do these people know that they are responsible? If not, can you help them to clarify their responsibilities?*
▶ *In a family, is it fair or appropriate for some of the responsibilities to be shared or negotiated between the adults and the children?*

What are the possible resolutions?

- ▶ *Are there resolutions that are win/win – they have the least drawbacks and give the most advantage to everyone?*
- ▶ *What might be the obstacles to these resolutions?*
- ▶ *How could the obstacles be overcome?*
- ▶ *How can everyone involved be supported when a resolution is not (or is only partly) achieved?*

Can they do it? Can you?

- ▶ *What skills and competences are needed?*
- ▶ *Do you have them? Do they? How could they be developed and supported?*
- ▶ *What can the other person learn in this situation? How can they be supported and developed?*

How do they react and respond?

- ▶ *What can you do to feel OK when the reactions are difficult and challenging?*
- ▶ *Can you do things differently so that the adults and children respond positively to the situation?*

Do they trust each other? And you?

- ▶ *How do you know?*
- ▶ *How can you build or rebuild trust in this situation?*

Index

Image credits